THE SPIRIT OF FINDHORN

THE
SPIRIT
OF
FINDHORN

Eileen Caddy

Preface, Introduction,
and Biography of the Author
by ROY McVICAR, *Member*
of the Findhorn Community

Published in San Francisco by
HARPER & ROW, PUBLISHERS
New York
Hagerstown
San Francisco
London

Line drawings by Daniel Marshall.
Photographs by Marion Stoker, Rod Thompson,
Thad Foulk, Kathy Thormod, Edwin Maynard,
and Kathleen Fekete.

LIBRARY OF CONGRESS CATALOG CARD NUMBER: 75-36747

ISBN: 0-06-061291-6

81 82 83 10 9 8 7 6 5 4

Contents

*I was shown the dawn of a glorious new day,
and was completely uplifted by the wonder
and beauty of it.*

*I heard the words: "This is but the dawn.
The day is even more wonderful,
more beautiful. Step into it,
and give eternal thanks now for all
that is waiting to unfold."*

Preface

EVERYWHERE IN THE WORLD we can see violence, poverty, injustice, and selfishness. And everywhere people are afraid, or bored, or unhappy, or filled with despair when faced with the futility of it all.

But underneath is a half-hope, seldom consciously expressed, that things need not be as they are; it is only a half-hope because most of us dare not really believe that the world can be transformed.

The Findhorn Community in northern Scotland is based on a strong faith that the world and people and living *can* indeed be different. And the Findhorn Community came into being because Peter and Eileen Caddy and their colleague, Dorothy Maclean, not only had that faith, but sought to act on it in their everyday lives and to demonstrate its reality and power for all people.

They did not set out to form a community. They simply believed that there is a divine plan for the world and that they were called to work together as part of that plan and to help usher in a New Age.

Living by that faith they found themselves guided to Findhorn. There with their three children they lived in a caravan (mobile home), learning to attune themselves ever closer to the God within and to live in harmony with the spiritual laws and truths revealed to them.

Eileen and Peter were perfectly suited to work together. Eileen spent hours each day listening to the inner voice teaching and guiding. Peter was the man of action and energy who gave the vision outward form and reality. The community has grown as others who shared their faith came to learn and live and serve the same divine purpose.

The truths that were communicated through Eileen are still a source of inspiration and power to the community, and her example has encouraged others to turn within to find their own guidance. The ideals embodied in Findhorn generate hope and give direction to people everywhere and point to what can be but the dawn of a glorious new day for mankind.

Introduction

FOR MANY YEARS Eileen Caddy (also known as Elixir) has listened in silence to the voice of God. The messages received give her explicit directions for her life, making God's plan for her and her husband, Peter, clear in detailed guidance, and opening up for her and for others the greater dimensions and wonders of living in the New Age. Eileen receives these transmissions in times of meditation and writes out in longhand the passages of guidance.

What kind of person is this who can experience such immediate contact with God? What is her background, and what has made her what she is now?

The biographical sketch that follows has been written in answer to these questions. It attempts to illuminate the meaning of Eileen's spiritual communications through an examination of her personal growth and development.

What emerges from the selected passages of guidance is the record of a unique and challenging way of life. Not poetry, yet not ordinary prose, Eileen's messages, in simple straightforward language, will illuminate and challenge you. These words are not the utterances of an armchair dreamer but come from one who has had to find her way in life step by arduous step. Each stage on the road of her spiritual growth was marked by hard and often bitter experiences.

Nothing has ever come easily to Eileen. What she is now: the love that others feel emanating from her and vibrating in her voice; the inner serenity that enables her to move quietly through the tasks and distractions of each day; the joy that sparkles in her eyes and ripples out in her laughter; the courage with which she faces an unpleasant interview or moves forward toward some new challenge—each of these qualities has been created in the rough and tumble of a tough and heartbreaking existence.

When Eileen's words are read quietly and receptively and, above all, when they are put to the only real test—that of action and practice—you discover to your surprise and perhaps exasperation that you are being invited to begin a new way of living. It is a way of life that not only challenges the materialism and selfishness of the world, but invigorates you with a new zest, as well as a deeper sense of purpose.

PART I

GLIMPSES OF EILEEN CADDY'S LIFE

I saw a potter molding what looked like a chalice, and I saw him mold and remold it until he was satisfied with the size and the shape. Then I saw him put it through all its various processes and right at the end when it seemed to be complete, it had either a crack or a flaw of some sort in it and it had to be cast out. With infinite patience he started again until he was completely satisfied with what he was making.

I heard the words: "Once I have laid My hand upon you I will never, never let you go until I have completed My handiwork. Be at perfect peace."

LITTLE IN EILEEN CADDY'S EARLY LIFE indicated that she would one day be the cofounder of a New Age spiritual community or that she would develop a unique power to hear and to share the voice of the God within.

She was born in Alexandria, Egypt, towards the end of the First World War, into a home where there was no outward allegiance to any church or religion. Her father had been brought up in a conventional Christian family and was taken to church three times every Sunday, as well as to Sunday School. When he grew up and married he determined not only to be free of this ritual himself but also not to impose it on his children.

Eileen along with her sister and brothers, therefore had no early religious training. Instead, Sundays were happy family days which parents and children spent together at home or at the seaside.

Her father was nonetheless a deeply spiritual man and had a thorough knowledge of the Bible. But more important, his life was a demonstration of Christian living. He and Eileen's mother were devoted to each other, and the home provided an atmosphere of true love and happiness.

When Eileen went to school at the age of six she received her first formal religious education. This, however, merely involved the memorization of selected passages from the Bible, and it made no apparent impact at all upon her growing mind or personality.

The first real crisis in Eileen's life occurred when she was sixteen. One day while she was at boarding school in England she was called to the headmistress's office. "Have you heard recently from your father?" asked the headmistress. "Yes," said Eileen. "Just a few days ago." "Well," the headmistress went on, "we have had a telegram saying that he has died." Eileen's reaction was disbelief. The headmistress showed her the telegram, but even when she read it Eileen still could not accept it. Her father, who was only forty-nine, had seemed to her too vital a person to die. Death simply could not touch him. It could not be final.

That is why she never shed a single tear for him even though she loved him dearly. Since the day she learned of her father's "death" Eileen has never had any fear of dying.

Her mother now felt that they should all be together as a family, and Eileen went back to Egypt to join the others. She became much more attached to her mother than before, feeling that her father would have wished that she take care of her. One of Eileen's brothers was an epileptic, and her mother had become an ardent Christian Scientist, hoping that through her faith her son might be healed. Eileen went with her to the Christian Science church but it made no deep impression on her.

She herself, however, did have a dramatic healing experience. After she had gone swimming in the Mediterranean Sea, at the time of the year it is polluted by the Nile flood, a spot on her forehead became inflamed and spread into a large suppurating sore. She was given healing by an uncle who was a Christian Science practitioner, and in a day or two the sore was completely healed.

This experience engendered within her a strong and deep belief in the power of mind over matter. As one of Eileen's messages states:

Love fulfills the law. Do you not realize that all the emotions opposite to Love violate the law and you work against all creation instead of with it? Your whole being is thrown out of alignment so that you are out of harmony with life, and when you are out of harmony your whole being reacts negatively. So often this is the cause of ill health. Change your thinking and you change your well-being.*

Eileen and her family went back to England after about a year in Egypt, and not long after that her mother died. Although she felt a deep sense of loss Eileen was able to pull through the experience of her mother's death without being shattered by it. Her next move was to take a course in domestic science, and when she completed this she took a job in an institution that operated as a preparatory school for part of the year and a holiday home for the rest.

After a year there, which passed without incident, her brother, who had been working in a bank, came to her with the suggestion that they use the money they had inherited to buy an inn. Since their epileptic brother was now in a special home and their younger sister was still at school, Eileen decided that she would fall in with his proposal. The inn was bought, and when war broke out in 1939 that is where she was.

Located in the country between Oxford and Banbury, the inn was frequented by Royal Air Force officers and men. Andrew Combe, one of the young officers, became Eileen's first husband. For some time their life together differed little from that of many other couples in the services during the war. One day, however, Andrew came home and told Eileen that he had met a man who had made a very profound impression on him. The man was a member of Moral Rearmament (MRA), a movement that teaches the Four Standards of Absolute Unselfishness, Absolute Purity, Absolute Love, and Absolute Honesty. Andrew suddenly found himself drawn to give his life fully to the movement.

At first Eileen was not particularly interested. She could not

---

* This passage and the others which follow, as well as the epigraph to this book and the epigraphs to the various sections, are selected from the guidance that Eileen Caddy receives in her times of meditation.

really understand Andrew when he talked about getting guidance from God. But she could see that her husband had changed a great deal, and on the whole had changed for the better. She went to London to meet others in MRA, but although she liked them and found them very kind, she had no real wish to get too involved in their organization. Andrew, however, was active in it, and Eileen saw clearly that the continued harmony of their life together would depend on her developing a sympathy for the movement.

It was thus because of her involvement in MRA that Eileen first attempted to "still herself" and listen to divine guidance. The experience, however, was not very real to her, and she often wrote something down just because it was expected of her. But she learned something of the intensity of self-searching, of ruthless honesty with oneself, and of the necessity of putting one's own life right before one could put the world right.

Yet she still remained somehow detached from it all. She went through the outward motions but was little changed inwardly. A great deal of what she saw in MRA she disliked and rejected. She felt that many of its tenets were grounded in self-righteous and rigid attitudes.

After the war Andrew was stationed in Iraq. Eileen and the children (there were now five) went with him. Unknown to any of them, this step into seemingly quiet waters was in fact a move into the outer edges of a veritable whirlpool.

As Eileen became increasingly dissatisfied with MRA, an inner hunger drew her, for the first time in her life, to the church. She took much pleasure in a job she had putting flowers in the church, and she would get up early in the morning in order to go to the first communion of the day. These activities met some inward need, though she hardly knew what it was; she only knew that they gave her comfort and a kind of joy.

Then one day Peter Caddy, a strange, serious young man,

came into her life. Andrew had invited Peter to dine at their home at the Habbaniya airbase in Iraq because he had been stimulated by an article Peter had written on leadership in the *RAF Quarterly*.

I saw a great many butterflies in a very beautiful garden. Then I saw that they were all flying towards one specific tree in the garden. This tree was covered with the most lovely blossoms, and I saw how the butterflies and the blossoms seemed to blend together perfectly.

I heard the words: "Behold like attracts like and becomes one."

Eileen had never met anyone like Peter before. He was attractive and vital, and there was a deep inner sense of purpose that showed in his every action and word, even in his eyes. Steeped as he was in esoteric and spiritual teachings and aware that he was preparing for some significant lifework, though as yet he did not know what it was, he talked and talked to her about things she simply could not understand.

But she was then, as now, a good listener!

It was not long, however, before the first signs began to show that there was more than a teacher/pupil relationship between them. At this time the cracks in Eileen's relationship with Andrew also became apparent. An officers' mess dance was scheduled to which she and Andrew were going, and Peter was to be there too.

For reasons she did not comprehend, Eileen decided to put on lipstick and makeup for the dance because she wanted to be as attractive as she could. However, makeup of any kind was strongly disapproved by MRA, and when they were ready to leave, Andrew asked her to remove it. Feeling an upsurge of independence, she refused. For the first time she was acting on her own.

Eileen had created a deadlock. Around midnight, Andrew realized that their absence from the dance would be difficult to explain and he decided they would go.

For Eileen this first step, albeit a small one, moved her towards a realization of her true self that was essential to her future. Again and again in later years she was to hear the inner Voice telling her to be herself:

Learn to stand on your own feet and be willing to step out bravely and take the consequences, no matter what they are likely to be. If you go through life depending on someone else, hoping to have your decisions made for you, refusing to stand on your own feet in case you make a mistake, you will never get anywhere.

You have to be strong and of good courage. You need to be willing to make mistakes and grow and learn as you do so. It does take courage and strength to do this, but a weakling will get nowhere.

Though she was not aware of it then, that incident on the night of the dance brought her one step nearer to Peter and the new and one step farther away from Andrew.

She saw Peter from time to time, though his RAF assignment often took him to other countries. Sometime later, when he had returned from a trip, he came to see her. They sat together on a couch, she at one end and he at the other. He began to tell her how, when he was in Jerusalem, he had climbed a hill and a revelation had come to him. It had been made unmistakably clear to him there that she, Eileen, was his other half; that they had a great work which they would do together, and at the right time God would bring them together.

Eileen had no idea whatsoever what Peter meant by her being his "other half," but she knew what would be involved in going away with him. She adamantly refused to go. Leave Andrew! Leave her children! Throw convention and respectability to the four winds! Incur the utter disapproval of society and be an outcast among her friends!

She could not imagine herself doing any of these things. At that point Peter had to take "no" for an answer. But he seemed in no way discouraged by her decision. He seemed to understand. He was prepared to wait; certain that when the time was right, she would be ready to come.

Soon after this Andrew decided that Eileen and the children should return to England without him, six weeks before his tour of duty in Iraq was over. Peter was delighted because, by divine intervention, he believed, he too was returning at the same time for a conference in London, and would be on the plane with Eileen. He would be able to look after her and help her.

Eileen panicked! She was only too well aware of what it might mean; she knew that the more they were together, the more they would be drawn to each other. She told Andrew that she wanted to delay her departure, but he advised that the arrangements had already been made. So she went, with Peter joining her en route.

Back in England Eileen settled in the country. One afternoon the telephone rang. It was Peter: "How about coming out to the theater?" Happily she agreed. They had dinner afterwards, and then went back to the country together.

And as Eileen so neatly puts it, "That was it." There was no hiding from the truth any longer. There could be no more pretending they were just friends. She knew now, as surely as did Peter, that their lives had merged and from now on their destinies were bound together.

Compelled by this unavoidable certainty Eileen had no more hesitation. She knew only too well what leaving Andrew for Peter would mean, but she also knew that she was both willing and able to face it. No matter what was involved, she could no longer "be satisfied to swim round and round in that little pool, safe and secure." She had to "be willing to swim out into the great wide ocean."

She wrote to Andrew, telling him that she loved Peter Caddy and that she wanted a divorce. Shortly after, she went with Peter to visit her sister in northern England for a few days, leaving the children at home with a friend, intending to return and await Andrew's reply. In the meantime Andrew had received her letter and had gotten special leave to return to England immediately. When he arrived, he asked Eileen not to return home or see the children.

Eileen was heartbroken but could not turn back now. The decision was hers. She and Peter had to move forward together into uncharted waters.

This experience taught Eileen a lesson she never forgot; in order to go forward into the new, there had to be a clear and clean break with the old. Many times through her inner guidance she was to share this awareness with others who were seeking to move into the New Age.

What a transformation it was for a girl who had grown up in such a conventional way, who had really only skimmed lightly over the surface of life. In one burst she shook off the shackles of tradition which were inhibiting the growth of her pioneering spirit, a spirit that was to develop into a force of inspiration for the New Age.

What are some of the qualities that characterize the pioneer impulse? *Courage? Faith? Independence?* Eileen surely had them in rich measure. Not that they were fully developed when she first joined Peter, but they were there. They had enabled her to take that essential first step without which no journey can begin.

Though mercifully she could not see ahead, she was destined to pass through many experiences and undergo changes which would test her qualities of strength to the utmost, and at the same time deepen them into an invincible power that would see her through it all, making her the light and inspiration she is now to growing numbers of people.

I was shown some well-worn cart ruts along a muddy road. There was a very heavy vehicle moving along the road which I saw sinking deeper and deeper into the mud, until finally it was firmly stuck and could not move.

I heard the words: "Move out of those well-worn ruts before it is too late, and you find yourselves firmly in them unable to move. Move into the glorious new."

The decision had been made. The crucial step had been taken. The break with the old had been finalized. Peter and Eileen now faced into the unknown.

They went to London to stay with Peter's wife, Sheena, a remarkable spiritual teacher. Before Peter had met Eileen, Sheena had said to him that she had been told by the divine power that communicated with her that she and Peter could no longer maintain their relationship as husband and wife, and that Peter should seek elsewhere for his true spiritual partner.

But although Peter and Sheena's marriage relationship was over, living with Sheena was hardly the happiest move for someone in Eileen's position. And Sheena was not the easiest nor the most congenial person to be with. She was inspired, yes; but she could also be ruthless in the discipline she imposed on those who were with her, as Peter knew only too well.

Understandably, Eileen was hardly ready to face the test of a confrontation with Sheena. She was shattered by the experience of parting with her children. She suffered the torment of guilt and felt that she really did not want to face anyone. If she could simply have been alone with Peter in some quiet place, to draw comfort and strength from their love and to find a new assurance in their oneness, she might quickly have come to feel that it was all worthwhile.

But the divine intelligence had a more gentle and wonderful way of unfolding its plan to her. Soon after coming to London, Eileen went with Sheena and Peter to Glastonbury, an ancient spiritual center, to seek direction in the decisions they had to make.

As she sat in the stillness of the sanctuary Eileen was led into a new and strange experience of God which was to change the whole course of her life and Peter's. It seemed that a stillness surrounded her and was matched by a deep peace within herself. In that stillness came words in a clear, calm yet authoritative voice: "Be still and know that I am God."

She sat on and listened. Again the Voice came, assuring her

that if she would always hear His words and follow step by step the guidance He gave, all would be well for her.

From that moment, sometimes uncertainly, sometimes unwillingly, Eileen has listened to that Voice and kept to the path it has shown. Peter had no doubts from the first. This was for him the supreme guide and he was ready to obey the words of counsel she received.

Eileen was led by the Voice to place herself in Sheena's hands for spiritual teaching and training, as Peter had done for five years. She did so, though she was not prepared for what that experience would demand of her. Peter had to return to the Middle East on business for the RAF, and so Eileen was alone—alone with Peter's wife to undergo a strenuous period of discipline which was the more intense because it had to be accomplished in a short time.

To say that she literally went through hell and found her slender inward strength stretched almost to the breaking point is an understatement. She has wondered many times, looking back, how she managed to avoid a complete breakdown! She feels that she survived only because through it all there was a greater plan operating and shaping her life, and because the inner Voice was always there to guide her, and because underneath were the everlasting arms.

For some months Sheena was ill, and Eileen had the unhappy task of nursing Peter's wife, a very trying patient. Sheena was in bed in an upstairs room; Eileen slept in a room directly beneath. There was a connecting telephone. At any time of day or night that telephone might ring and Eileen would have to go up to Sheena, who was irritable and even cruel in her suffering. Sheena might demand, "Give me healing." And Eileen who knew nothing about healing would just kneel there by the bedside, hold her hands over the place where the pain was, and pray.

She often had to remain in that position for hours on end, not daring to move, until every muscle and nerve in her body was crying for relief.

Nor could Peter give her much comfort when he was at home, for he knew why she had to endure this and could only tell her that it was a necessary part of her training for their future work together.

Many a time it must have seemed to Eileen that since she had made the break she had taken one blow after another. But in later years, after she had come through it all, she could see the purpose running through her trials and understand the lessons she had learned and the insights they had brought. As a result of her own suffering she could understand what others suffered and could enter into their distress and bring the guidance and encouragement they needed. But the true source of her strength came from the inner Voice which spoke to her:

Do you feel the burden you are carrying is too heavy, that you have been given far too great a task to carry out and you long to run away from it all and be free from it? Why not start right now to cast all your burdens and cares upon Me and let Me navigate you through these troublesome waters? I know the way, for I am the way, the truth, and the life. I will pilot you through every difficulty into calm and still waters, and free you from every strain, when your faith and trust are wholly in Me.

Perhaps the most difficult lesson she had to learn, the one Sheena was determined she and Peter should both learn, was that God must be put first in their lives. Before children, before home, before each other—God must come first.

Had Eileen not known by this time the inner Voice guiding, comforting, and encouraging her, she could never have met that supreme challenge. There were times when she almost lost the Voice, times when she would hear it and doubt its truth, times when it was confused among many other voices. But always when she most desperately needed it, it would ring out again in the inner sanctuary.

And how often through the years it recalled her to the heights of God's vision for her life, recalled her to the necessity of putting Him before all else.

13

I need you free, not all tied up with self and self-concern. I do ask for everything; there can be no holding back anything. I know what is best for each one of you, therefore let Me guide you so that you are always in the right place at the right time. Seek My guidance every step of the way. Never forget to put first things first. Put Me first in everything then nothing can go wrong.

These were lessons learned through the discipline of suffering, and they were lessons learned well.

After many ups and downs, many twistings and turnings, they were in truth piloted into calmer waters. Peter resigned his commission in the Royal Air Force and they were guided to a job together, he as a gardener and she as kitchen maid at a school in Southern England. It was there, with Peter and Eileen's second child coming, that they bought the caravan that would one day be their only home.

Eileen's greatest suffering, now that they were together and away from Sheena, was a profound and inescapable feeling that she was "living in sin." She had left her legal husband, deserted her children, lost her friends, and was now living with a married man. It was nothing less than an agony of shame to her.

She could not help looking back and thinking of her beloved father. He and her mother had truly loved each other. They had given her the ideal of what a home should be, with love and loyalty and unfailing trust. She had grown up with the idea of marriage as a lifelong state; no notion of divorce had entered into it. And all this intensified her guilty conscience and her unhappiness, depression, and remorse.

Years were to pass before Eileen was able to achieve freedom from this complex emotional distress, and to experience the soothing and healing of those savage wounds to her soul. But looking at it through the perspective of time, she can see at least two compensations that emerged from her time of distress which have contributed to the work she is doing now.

One is a great gain in compassion and understanding. It has made her sympathetic toward other women who have found themselves in similar circumstances. When one of her unmarried daughters wrote to her after sixteen years of silence to say that she was pregnant, Eileen, without hesitation, asked her to come and visit. In the letter, her daughter explained that the man did not want to get married, but despite the suggestions of friends to the contrary, she wanted the baby.

After she arrived the father of the unborn child came to visit her at the community before going abroad. While there he had a change of heart and the couple decided to get married. Their decision brought Andrew, Eileen's ex-husband, to Scotland for the wedding. This was a big step toward the eventual reconciliation of the family. Eileen had had guidance years before that at the right time she would be reunited with all her children and her ex-husband in love and harmony. Eileen's first grandchild was born at Findhorn and the new family remained in the community for fourteen months before setting off for the son-in-law's home abroad.

One by one Eileen has been reunited with all her children, but it took seventeen years for this to come about. The important lesson of patience had to be learned: man's timing is not necessarily God's. (Recently Eileen and Peter have returned to the Cluny Hill Hotel, which has been bought by the Findhorn community. Peter was manager of the Cluny Hill, a large, luxury hotel in nearby Forres in northern Scotland, before he and Eileen came to Findhorn. God had promised them that "after a bit longer" they would once again be running the hotel. It took fourteen years until it happened.)

The other compensation she gained from her experience is even more far-reaching. The New Age will certainly involve breaking away from the ideas and customs that have ceased to have any real meaning today. In particular this is true of notions about sex and marriage; for so often people marry because they believe they are in love, but after some years stay together only because of convention or respectability or concern for what people might say.

Laws and standards imposed on life from outside are losing their validity and those who would move into the New Age must learn to move from obeying the law into being the law.

One vital aspect of this New Age living is liberation from the legalistic approach to human behavior, and from the sense of guilt which an act in defiance of traditional "laws" engenders. It was only after many unhappy years that Eileen attained this freedom and was able to share her insights with others whose needs were like her own.

> In the New Age it is not necessary to wear sackcloth and ashes. It is not necessary to go around declaring that you are a miserable sinner and are not worthy to be called My beloved child.
>
> All this is of the old and is false and unreal. Accept that we are one, that I am within each one of you. Feel yourselves being lifted out of the darkness of all this false teaching into the glorious light. Leave behind all the old. Let it die a natural death, and enter the new reborn in spirit and in truth, and know the meaning of true freedom.

It might have seemed that after all she had been through, Eileen had reached the state of attunement for which she was destined. But she had one final depth to plumb in her struggle before reaching that state. This came when Sheena, who was now staying in a summer cottage on a bleak island off Scotland, wanted to see Eileen and Peter's children. Eileen and the children went alone, and the months that followed were to Eileen a veritable "dark night of the soul."

Those who have gone through the darkness of such an experience know that it is both sacred and unique. What matters most in Eileen's case is that she came through it with a stronger faith in God, a greater assurance that He was always with her and would guide her step by step to fulfill His perfect plan, a deeper and wider love for all people, and the burning conviction that it was in her own hands to follow the way that would bring joy and peace into her life.

She had still a long way to go. But the darkness was breaking, and the light was growing brighter with every step.

> I was shown two baby chicks hatching out of their shells. I saw one being helped, and when it was taken out of its shell and put on the ground it was so weak and feeble that it did not survive long. The other one I saw working really hard to free itself of its shell, and when it emerged it was strong.

> I heard the words: "Be willing to do your own spiritual work, to find your own strength within so you are strong and whole and are able to survive the stresses and strains of the world."

Biographies of mystics and spiritual leaders through the ages teem with accounts of dramatic events that were turning points in their lives. Very often these incidents led to a complete change in their way of living, or at least to a new awakening to the reality of the spiritual world. From that point they set out on a new life which they believed to be their true destiny.

This is true of Moses at the burning bush, of Samuel hearing God calling to him by name, of Paul on the Damascus Road coming face to face with the Christ, of St. Francis, Luther, Wesley; the list is endless. The nature of these experiences and the forms they take are as varied as the men and women who have them. Eileen's experience came in the small sanctuary at Glastonbury, and it had the same vivid and dramatic quality as have those of other spiritual leaders. She heard the divine Voice speaking with unmistakable authority and power, "Be still and know that I AM GOD."

What could it mean? She was not equipped to understand such an experience. For her quiet and conventional upbringing had never led her to believe God would speak to people directly. In the Bible, yes. In church, perhaps. But not to someone who was neither spiritually oriented, nor wished to be so. Yet to her—a moral and social rebel—God spoke. And His word set her on the road that eventually led to her cofounding the Findhorn Community with Peter.

It was a long, rough, winding road. Slowly, steadily she became more and more sure of her guidance. She was able to hear the Voice more clearly. She and Peter came to follow its instructions more and more implicitly, even in the most practical details of their everyday living.

With many, many people Eileen has shared the secret which she has learned: that the only way to find peace and happiness and live a fulfilling life is to be willing to change—change one's thinking, change one's way of life, change one's consciousness. "Let go and simply follow My instructions step by step, and you will see miracle upon miracle take place in your lives and living."

As Peter and Eileen learned to make contact with God and seek guidance every step of the way, they learned that it worked, that doors would open and changes would come and miracles would happen. They were led from one place to another, coming at last to Glasgow where they were married. While they were there, they got a job that was to have great significance for them. Peter was appointed manager of the Cluny Hill Hotel.

They ran this busy concern obeying God's guidance in every detail. If some problem came up that Peter felt he could not handle, he would go straight to Eileen and she would drop everything in order to seek guidance.

After five years there and a year at another hotel in Scotland they found themselves out of work, with no place to stay, puzzled that divine guidance should work in such devious ways. They then made the move which is now widely known; they went back to their caravan, which was sited at Findhorn, and brought it to the very last place they would ever have chosen, a dirty, windswept corner of Findhorn Bay Caravan Park, because that was where God said to go.

The story of what happened in the years after that is told in *The Magic of Findhorn, The Findhorn Garden,* and in other books. What we are concerned with here, however, is Eileen—a woman who can hear the Voice of God, not in profound mystic truths, but in simple, practical, day-to-day directions. The evolution of the Findhorn Community cannot be explained but for these eminently pragmatic words.

Is Eileen then unique? Has she a very special spiritual quality that sets her apart? Is hers a special gift possessed and used by a unique person to accomplish a specific task?

Eileen would pronounce an unequivocal no to these questions. Anyone, she affirms over and over again, can receive clear guidance if he will learn to be still and to listen and obey. "Everyone may not hear that 'still small voice' as clearly as I do, but why not try to see what happens when you learn to be still and listen? Maybe you will hear something, maybe you will be aware of some action to be taken, maybe intuitively you will know what to do. Unless you try it you will never know whether it works or not. Be patient, persist, persevere, and I know you will be rewarded. Then try to live by it."

At the same time, however, there is a unique quality in Eileen. As she herself has said many times, each one of us is unique and has his or her own special contribution to make to the whole. And Eileen has her own particular part, which no one else can fill. Through the ordeals of preparation, through hard years of training and discipline, through countless failures and mistakes and persistent learning from those mistakes, she has attained a great clarity of mind and a transparent purity of being which makes her a very special instrument of the Divine for the perfecting of His plan for mankind.

It will be worthwhile at this point to look at some of the highly individual and distinctive features of her messages and the style in which they are written. She, of course, will say that these are the words as she hears them; they are not her own. God speaks through her. But He uses her mind on various levels, and therefore the messages are shaped and colored by the nature of her mind and experience.

One obvious quality of the messages is their simplicity. They never partake of complex intellectualizing, complicated phraseology, or excess verbiage. The truths are direct and practical, the words simple and concise, and it is this which gives them their universal appeal. The value of simplicity was often stressed by the inner Voice:

> The hallmark of truth is simplicity. It is My hallmark, printed indelibly on everything that is of Me. Look at the beauty and simplicity of nature. When a child looks at a flower he does not waste time wondering how it came about but looks at its color and shape in sheer joy and wonderment. He bends down and puts his little face to it, drinking in the glory of its perfume. He does not stop to wonder where the perfume comes from or how it was created, but accepts it all as the most natural thing in the world, a gift which has been given to him to enjoy. Why not accept the wonder and simplicity of life and not try to work out the complexity of it all with the mind. Keep it simple.

Yet quite a profound truth is often clothed in vivid, even surprising images. For instance, about living the spiritual life the guidance she received says: "When you want to reach the top of a ladder you have to put your foot on the first rung and pull yourself up to the next one and so on. You will never reach the top of a ladder by just standing at the bottom of it looking up." Again, stressing the need to keep trying, she was told: "Be like an India rubber ball; keep bouncing up and up, never allowing yourself to be kept down." Sometimes her images may startle us by their commonplaceness: "When you have an ingrowing toenail, it hurts. When a soul is ingrowing and fails to give out, fails to expand, that soul suffers much pain and conflict." The sheer surprise in such analogies has the effect of sharply awakening the mind.

Also the very simplicity of her words may carry a direct challenge. There is no pulling of punches, no sugar-coating of the pill. What she receives comes in a straight and blunt way:

"This life is not for weaklings." "Never be a slave to time." "It is so easy to slam the door on truth because it is revealed through some unusual and unorthodox means." One may not be comfortable with what she hears, may doubt that it comes from God, but a person cannot escape the challenge of it or evade its implication for his or her life.

At the very core of this study of Eileen, as it is at the very core of her experience, is a very daunting question. What of the God who speaks? Who is this God?

As man evolved through the ages, so have his ideas and his experiences of that God. To primitive man God was completely "Other," a being so different and so distant that man could have no direct experience of Him. Indeed, one of his greatest fears was that he might "see" God.

So God was either removed to a distant heaven, or to another realm where man would not know Him until after death. One way or another He was removed to a "safe distance."

As man's experience grew, so gradually God became more accessible, more approachable, more lovable; until at last communication with a separate God developed into communion with Him and finally became union with Him. God and man knew and expressed their oneness.

Eileen has been aware of a similar process of growth and increasing intimacy in her relationship with the Divine. She writes:

> Life is a process, a constant process of change; and as my consciousness and concepts of God began to grow and change, so did my understanding. What I saw through a glass darkly I began to see more clearly. The Voice I first heard I accepted as from the Lord God. He became the Father to a beloved child, guiding and directing that child.
>
> But gradually the relationship to the Divine changed and became as a marriage to the Beloved. There is no longer any separation because one knows the Oneness with the Divinity within, the Oneness with all Life.

In trying to clarify the concept of the God within, the young writer and lecturer David Spangler, a member of the Findhorn Community for three years and founder of the Lorian Association, carefully avoided making any statement that could evolve into just another formal doctrine. As he put it, "We believe that each individual must find God in his own way, and we recognize that God has as many infinite aspects as there are individuals to relate to Him." Any attempt to lay down final statements about God or how one should relate to Him serves only to limit Him and make a truly creative experience of Him impossible.

We cannot sum up this same facet of Eileen's experience in better words than those of David's: "I know that Elixir is indeed in communication with God—not a god of a particular religion, not a god of a particular sect or creed, but the God who throughout all time and in all situations is the source of that life, wisdom, inspiration, clarity of perception and right action which allows life to unfold freely and transcendentally."

> I was shown seaweed floating in the sea and I could see its grace of movement, its beauty of shape and color. Then I was shown it washed up on the rocks, where it lay becoming hard and brittle, losing all its beauty and color for it was out of its element.

> I heard the words: "Find your rightful element in your Oneness with Me. Find your true beauty and freedom doing My Will and walking in My ways, and be at perfect peace."

If one thing more than another proved that Eileen and Peter were being guided by a higher Power and not just following their own wishes, it is that they came to stay at Findhorn Bay Caravan Park. For who would ever have chosen to make their home there with three young children? And who could have thought it a good idea to make that flat stretch of gorse-covered sand the setting for a spiritual community?

It would not have been surprising had they questioned this particular bit of guidance. Or perhaps wondered if they had heard the Voice correctly. It would have been very natural if they had found the move difficult to understand. So Eileen was told rather bluntly more than once: "Why waste time trying to work out the rhyme and reason for everything? My ways are not man's ways, therefore it is a complete waste of time and energy trying to work them out with the mind. Simply be willing to accept them and give eternal thanks for them, enjoying life to the full."

So they stayed! Day after day, week after week. The details of the story are now widely known: how the miraculously fecund garden was gradually established on previously barren ground, how people came one by one to join them, how the buildings and the different departments of the community came into being, all following the specific directions given to Eileen each day in guidance.

Peter was unswerving in his positive faith and absolute confidence that God was leading them and that this was somehow the work they had to do. As soon as Eileen had a clear vision of the next phase in the growth of the community, Peter went right ahead to give it form. The messages of these visions often seemed absurd by the standards of human perception; for example, the one that led them to build a new kitchen. The Voice directed them to construct a kitchen that would serve two hundred people, when there were only about twelve in the group. But Peter went ahead in faith, and now the kitchen is stretched to capacity to provide for the community and guests.

As the various sections of the community came into being— the office, kitchen, printing, and so on—messages came to Eileen regarding each of them, and it was part of her special function to keep the vision clear. It was quite simply that nothing less than the very best was good enough for God. There must be nothing second-rate about the equipment they bought, and nothing slipshod in the work that was done. "Never be satisfied with second best. Always remember that all you are doing is for Me and to My honor and glory, therefore only the very best will do. Your only desire is for the very best for your Beloved."

Constantly, through the years of growth and changing personnel, Peter and Eileen have had to keep this standard true and make sure that new members were given the same vision. Peter had to make certain that other people did not distort the original vision with their own pet ideas concerning how the development of the community should be realized while Eileen held the vision clear and steady. This was especially true when the sanctuary was to be built.

In the early days the family met morning and evening for meditation in their own caravan. As their numbers grew another caravan was set aside for this purpose. In time Eileen received guidance that a special sanctuary should be built. Before plans for its construction had been formulated a number of people who came to Findhorn professed that they knew what form it should take. One after another contributed his vision for it, until there were so many ideas that the whole community was in total confusion about the project.

Then Eileen was given a definite description of what God wanted; a plain cedarwood building, with no symbols and no elaborate decoration. Simplicity and beauty were to be its keynotes. So all other plans were set aside, and this was the one that was built.

At first, when Eileen, Peter, their children, and Dorothy Maclean were alone at Findhorn, they had not yet been given a clear idea of what they were to be doing. They knew that God had brought them there and they knew He had some plan for them and a work for them to do. But what? All they could do was live one day at a time and wait for the vision to be revealed.

But as time went on Eileen found that the guidance concerning the work they had to do at Findhorn began to become clear. In the beginning they had felt that what they were doing in that out-of-the-way corner of the caravan park had no significance beyond themselves. Even when numbers grew and the community developed it still seemed to them to be just a personal venture of faith. But again and again they were told: "What you are doing is far greater than you realize." They gradually came to understand that one day what they were building would have world-wide repercussions, and that they were no less than pioneers of a New Age for mankind.

A truly audacious faith to hold at that time!

Another truth that was strongly emphasized in their early guidance was that each person, even in the small group, has a special part to play in working out the divine plan for the whole. As far back as 1963 this was made clear to Eileen:

> Unity in a group is vitally important. You each have to learn to work together like the fingers on a hand. You each have your different roles, and remember they are entirely different; so you need never try to copy anyone else. You are all individuals very specially chosen and trained by Me to do a specific work which only you can do. You can each help each other when help is needed, but the actual work has to be done by you.

This was true even when there were only a dozen in the group. How much more essential and challenging this notion became when there were two hundred people of different races and cultures and backgrounds living together. So often the guidance of early days gained in force and relevance as time went on.

As more and more people came to join the community, the greater was the need for them to share the vision of Findhorn, to raise their consciousnesses to that level of positive faith which Eileen and Peter had had to reach. Everyone had to learn to blend their differences in unity.

Some found the challenge too great and left. Some found it relatively easy to be open and make the changes involved. Others needed help in experiencing change and here too Eileen had an invaluable part to play.

Since she lives on a unique level of communion with God, Eileen has her very own way of helping people. She is, of course, a good listener. She does not just hear what you are saying; she *listens to you*. And she is not only sympathetic and receptive but often very positive and challenging in her pronouncements.

Eileen also helps people during her times of quiet meditation. If there is someone who she knows is in special need of help, she will bring that person into her meditation, see him surrounded with light, and then quite simply pour love out to him. Many have experienced great spiritual transformation as a result of this, though they often do not know what caused it.

One key to a deeper understanding of Eileen is in the name by which she is also known, Elixir. The name was given to her not long after her first experience of hearing the divine Voice at Glastonbury. Sitting one day in silence she felt, rather than saw, the word *Elixir* as if it were branded on her forehead. But it had no clear meaning for her then, and for some years she forgot about it.

As she became more intimate with her inner Voice, she asked what her spiritual name was. The answer came with unmistakable clarity, *Elixir*. "The individual name, when rightly understood, is a passage in the Book of Life which meaneth all things to the one so described, and without the knowledge of which he cannot serve God to the best of his ability." Asking for more enlightenment about the meaning of Elixir, she was told:

> Your true name *Elixir* is described as *Eternal Life,* which means you are and you radiate forth *eternal life* bringing this truth to mankind:
>
> to bring belief to the unbeliever
> to bring hope to the hopeless
> to bring healing to those who faint along the way
> to bring comfort to those who sorrow and are brokenhearted
> to bring love to the unloved and despised.
>
> Stretch out and expand. There is no limitation in the expansion,

no limitation to the vastness of your work. With the expansion I give you the help, the understanding, the illumination; therefore now you do indeed serve *Me* to the best of your ability, Elixir My beloved child.

This was the fulfillment of the promise: "This is My name for you. I have bestowed it upon you. I have blessed you with it. There is a deep spiritual meaning to it which gradually you will come to understand." The work Eileen is doing at Findhorn, the role she is able to play with ever-increasing effectiveness and fulfillment is but the unfolding of her true inner potential and the ever-deepening realization of her name.

Elixir is a spiritual descendant of true visionaries and mystics of all the ages, whatever their spiritual heritage. Her experience of God has the same profound yet progressive quality; her communion with the Divine has the same transparent certainty.

But she is no unpractical dreamer. She lives a full life amid the realities of a busy home, the center of an ever-changing community. She is to be found not only in the sanctuary, but in the kitchen preparing a meal for two hundred people, or in her bungalow being hostess to members and guests.

As she has developed spiritually, as the inner voice has come to her ever more clearly, ever more strongly, as her contact with the Divine has deepened and her response to Him has become more immediate and complete, there has yet been no tendency for her experience of Him—wonderful and intimate as it is—to become a luxury; it has never become overly ecstatic or emotional or out of touch with real life.

On the contrary her communication with the Divine has had an ever closer impact on her life in the world. The God within her has always insisted that life led in obedience to His guidance is a life of action. It is a life of demonstration. It must express itself in the way one works. One must labor not only with love but with the knowledge that only a perfect job is good enough for God. A person who lives in obedience to divine inspiration must express a new quality of love in his relationships with people, a love that knows no limitations, admits no barriers, and tolerates no exceptions. The whole of one's life, from morning to night, must be such that it reflects the freedom and beauty and joy of the divine Life.

The great scientist and seer, Pierre Teilhard de Chardin, though of a very different spiritual tradition, would have found in Elixir a kindred spirit, for he insisted on the same challenging integration of the spiritual life and everyday life. He put it this way:

> God, in all that is most living and incarnate in Him, is not far away from us, altogether apart from the world we see, touch, hear, smell, and taste about us. Rather He awaits us every instant in our action, in the work of the moment. There is a sense in which He is at the tip of my pen, my spade, my brush, my needle—of my heart and of my thought. By pressing the stroke, the line, or the stitch on which I am engaged to its ultimate natural finish, I shall lay hold of that last end toward which my innermost will tends. (*The Divine Milieu*, pp. 36–7.)

In her everyday life, Elixir manifests her vision through constant commitment to far-reaching change in our way of living. "This is a life of change."

There was no chance, following the inner voice, of slipping into the New Age carrying over the vestiges of old ways of thinking, old attitudes to life, or old habits and patterns of reaction. The One whose voice is heard in the stillness is the One who says, "Behold, I make all things new."

And change can be uncomfortable. Many will try every means available to avoid it.

> Let there be no complacency. For when you are complacent you can so easily get into a rut, which creates stagnation. See where you need to change and then take the action necessary to bring about that change. If change is uncomfortable, the more quickly it takes place the easier it is. It is far less painful to pull a bandage off quickly than to do it slowly. Therefore do what you know has to be done without wasting any time thinking

about it and wondering about it. Take that leap into the New without hesitation and simply know that it will be wonderful, far more wonderful, than what you have left behind in the old.

With change comes life, a full and glorious life.

This is, in fact, the only way we can help to bring about the New Age. By starting with ourselves. According to the way we live our lives, we are either part of the world's problem or part of its solution.

Eileen has had to work through much herself; the transformations in her life have been arrived at through adversity and she often has had to submit to trials that required every ounce of faith and courage and dedication she could muster. She never stands still, but is always moving forward towards ever greater heights. It is for these reasons that Eileen is never a sentimental companion; she is ever ready to call out the best in those around her, because she sees only the very best in them.

I saw the most glorious sunrise from the top of a mountain. I longed for it to remain, and that I could remain in that state of ecstasy forever.

But I heard the words: "Things are changing all the time. You cannot remain on the mountaintop all your life. Come down into the valley, and live a life, and reflect the beauty and wonders that have been shown you in your life and living, so that I may be glorified."

An experience Eileen had several years ago was a highlight of vision for her and throws some illumination on the inner reality of her soul. It is an essential fact of this experience that it is linked both with a deep transformation in her life and with a going forth to a life of demonstration and activity.

To present the account of this experience in Eileen's own words is the best way to communicate its truth and power.

First Day

The first morning I went to the sanctuary I was not as early as I should have been. Some members of the community were there before me. I sat down and felt great peace and oneness.

Then most unexpectedly the top of the record player fell down with a crash. It was such a shock it seemed to shatter every nerve in my being. I burst into tears, shaking all over.

Two persons came and assured me that all was well. I knew it was, but I was not prepared for such shock treatment. After that a great peace descended upon me.

It seemed as if I had to have this shock to open up everything in me.

Second Day

The next morning I went in to the sanctuary really early, before anyone else had arrived. As I sat down I was told to sound the OM. It was something I had not done for a very long time, but I did what I was told and sounded it five times.

Then as I sat quietly, it was as if the top of my head opened up and light was being poured into my whole being. It could not be contained, so it flowed out of my fingertips and toes.

Third Day

This morning I again got to the sanctuary early, and again I was told to sound the OM.

Again the tremendous pure light and energy poured through the opening on the top of my head and through my whole being. But this time it was so great that it flowed through every atom of my being, out and out.

Then I seemed to be suffocating. It was as if there was something deep in my being trying to be released. I could not breathe and I started to get frightened.

These words came to me: *"Let go, and go with all that is taking place."* This is not easy to do when you are struggling for breath; but I let go, and the thing within me came up and up, and a white dove flew out of my head and flew away.

I heard the words, *"I am free, free, free."* I felt a wonderful sense of freedom.

Fourth Day

This morning I followed the same instructions about sounding the OM. It was made clear to me that the reason for this was to raise my vibrations. I had thought it was to raise the vibrations in the sanctuary.

Again the tremendous pure light and energy poured through and out of every atom of my whole being. Then my being seemed to undergo a strange transformation. For a second I was really afraid, but the words came to me, *"Be afraid of nothing. Go with all that is taking place."*

My being seemed to become the earth, and it was terribly battered and bruised. Then a terrible pain went through me. It was so bad I thought something awful was happening to me. I remembered the words, *"I am with you always."* So I just let go completely and allowed things to happen.

When the pain became so bad that I felt I could take no more, I felt it being very gently and lovingly pushed towards the sun; and the nearer it got to the sun the less it became, until it entered right into the sun and became nothing. Yet it became everything because it was one with *all*.

And I heard the words: *"The earth and all humanity made new."*

Fifth Day

On the last morning I went to the sanctuary early, and I was taken aback when I found a strange young man sitting in the chair just behind mine.

I knew I had to sound the OM, but did not know what to do about it. So I leant back and put my hand on the young man's knee and just told him I was going to sound the OM and for him not to be disturbed.

After I had done this I again experienced the tremendous pure light and energy pouring through my whole being and out of every atom. I felt as if my being was a transformer for the pure light and energy to flow through and out to those who where not ready to receive the pure light directly.

Then it was as if my skin was being peeled off me. It started from the opening at the top of my head and was slowly peeled off the whole of me, right off my toes, and was cast in front of me.

As I looked at it, it appeared to be like the skin a snake had shed, and it lay there shrivelling up into nothingness.

I knew then what it was to be a being of light, and I heard the words:

"Now go forth, and be my light, my love, my wisdom."

PART II

WORDS TO LIVE BY

I was shown a great ball of light. Coming from it were bright rays of light and going back into it were dull rays. I wondered what was happening, then I heard the words: "Be at peace. When you have been the full cycle, you will return to Me, the Source of all life, of light, and you will become one with Me as you were in the beginning."

The Dawn Is at Hand

I was shown a very dark night unfolding into the most glorious day. I saw how it had to go through different stages before it reached the final one.

I heard the words: "Fear not the darkness, but know that the dawn is near at hand and out of the dawn shall emerge a glorious new day. Hold on, hold on in faith and faint not along the way."

The key to your happiness and contentment lies deep within
    each one of you,
Within your own hearts and minds.

The way you start each day is very important
You can start off on the right foot or the wrong.
You can wake up with a song of joy and gratitude in your
    hearts
For the new day,
For being alive,
For the very wonder of living
And of being in tune and harmony with the rhythm of all life.

You can expect the very best from the coming day
And therefore draw it to you;
Or you can start the day with a chip on your shoulder,
Really disgruntled and out of rhythm.
It all rests with you.
You cannot blame your state of mind on anyone else.

Because yesterday was not all it should have been does not
    matter:
Yesterday is finished and gone
You cannot do anything about it.
Today is a completely different matter;
It lies before you, untouched and unblemished
It is up to you to make it the most wonderful day.
It is up to you to choose what today is going to be
And then make it so.

How do you start off each day?
Remember it is no concern of anyone else.
This is something you and you alone have to choose to bring
    about.
This is where self-discipline comes in.
Try to start the day off with inner peace and contentment,

By taking time to be still
And allowing that peace to infill and enfold you.

Take time to get into tune
And do not rush into the day unprepared and out of harmony.
If you do
It is so easy to take that state of mind into the day,
Allowing it to affect the whole of the day and all those you
    contact.

You are responsible for what today will bring.
Knowing this gives you an even greater responsibility than
    those souls who are not aware of it
And therefore know no better.
From those to whom much is given, much is expected.

I pour down My blessings and My gifts upon each one of you.
You are all fully aware of this
And therefore you are open and ready to accept them or reject
    them.
It is simply up to you.

There are many, many souls who are not aware of this,
Who go through life completely blind
To all the wonderful things there are around and within them.
They are still asleep spiritually
And in that state miss much.

The way you live,
The way you are,
May help to awaken some slumbering soul,
So always give of your very best wherever you are
Or wherever you go
And so allow yourselves to be used to help your fellowman
Not by many words,
But by the way you live.

Words can create harmony and peace
And awaken a soul to the things that really matter in life.

Only feed spiritual food to those who are ready for it
And then only a little at a time.
"Seek and ye shall find" is a law,
Therefore let those who long to find seek and seek
And their deep inner longings will be answered.

It is easy enough to love
When everything is going smoothly in your lives.
It is when you find yourselves up against things
That you are inclined to close your hearts
And stop the flow of love
Yet this is the time when the need for the flow of love is even
     greater.

Can you truly love
When you are beset by tests and trials
And you feel everything and everyone is against you?
When you can do this
And there is no hardness or bitterness in you,
When the love is flowing despite all outer conditions,
Then you can be sure it is indeed My Divine Love
Which is flowing in and through you
And that that wondrous love will win through in the end.

Love goes on and on
And never gives up;
It will try one way
And then another,
Until it wins through.

Love is gentle
And yet strong and persistent.
It is like water,
It wears a way through to the very hardest of hearts.
So love and keep on loving,
And watch the way open up
And never accept no for an answer.

"Blessed are they which do hunger and thirst after
    righteousness
For they shall be filled."

When your longing is strong enough it will be fulfilled,
For you will search and search for the answer
And will not be satisfied until you have found it.
You will have the determination and patience,
Perseverance and persistence
To leave no stone unturned
Until you have found what you are looking for along this
    spiritual path
Which is your realization of Oneness with Me.

Never be disheartened
Or feel you are chasing the end of a rainbow,
But simply know that you will find what you are looking for
    in the end
If you do not faint along the way
Or give up in despair.

As every obstacle along the way is worth overcoming
To reach the goal,
Be determined to find the way around it
And never at any time feel anything is insurmountable or
    impossible.

"Be strong and of good courage"
Go on and on
And you will surely get there.
When you are going through a long dark tunnel
You can see that tiny glow of light at the far end,
You will never give up until you reach it.
No matter how hard the going may be,
You know the end is in sight

And every step you take no matter how small takes you
    nearer
Ever nearer that wonderful glow of light at the end.

Do not falter,
Keep on
And keep the goal in sight all the time.

Love will always find a way.
Love will give you the strength to go on,
So keep the love flowing
And never close your hearts when the going gets very
    tough and rough
And everything seems to be against you.

THE UNIQUENESS OF EACH PERSON

Always remember you are a unique individual
And have a unique gift to give to the whole.
You may not have discovered that gift yet,
Therefore take time to search your hearts and your
    lives
And find out what it is.
When you have found it
Then use it unhesitatingly for the whole.

Never try to compare your gift with anyone else's.
Simply accept it as yours.
Give thanks for it
And see how wonderfully it works.

Why wish you were someone else
Or wish you had someone else's gift?
It is such a waste of time and energy
And will only make you really frustrated
And dissatisfied with yourselves and with life.

You have within you all that you need,
So you do not have to waste time searching for it
    without.
That unique gift is hidden deep within you
Waiting there to be drawn forth
When you are ready to recognize
And use it for the benefit of the whole.

What is your gift?

Never get depressed or discouraged
Because you feel you are not advancing very fast along this
    spiritual path.
Why not take a look backwards
And see how far you have come?
When you do this
You will be surprised to find the tremendous changes and
    growth
Which have taken place.

Always try to think the very best about yourselves,
Not the worst as some of you are inclined to do.
I AM within you,
Therefore when you belittle yourselves,
You belittle Me.
Have you ever thought of that?
If not, it is high time you did.

You can do all things with Me,
For with Me nothing is impossible.
Never fail to give Me the honor and glory,
Never fail to recognize My hand in everything
And give eternal thanks for everything I bestow upon you.
You would not be where you are,
Doing what you are doing at this time
If I had not laid My hand upon you.

See a perfect pattern and plan running through your lives.

There is nothing haphazard,
Even though it may appear to be very strange.
All is in My Divine Plan.

My ways are not man's ways.
You may wander off the straight and narrow path at times
But sooner or later you will come back onto it again.
Seek always to do My will no matter what the cost.
I know what is best for you
So why fight against it
And think that you know best?
You can waste so much precious time when you do this.

Have absolute faith and trust in Me
And know that I will never let you down nor forsake you,
That I am always there.

Keep turning to Me,
Listen to what I have to say to you in the silence
And obey My slightest whisper,
For obedience opens up a whole new life for you
And releases new energies which have been hidden deep
        within you,
Waiting to be released at the right time,
When you were ready
And responsive
And willing to follow them out without question or
        query.
They are too powerful to be released
Until all has been prepared and made ready.

THE SIMPLICITIES OF LIFE

Keep life as simple as possible
And enjoy to the full the simple things all around you,

The simple wonders and beauties which are there for all to
    share
But which are so often taken for granted because they are
    missed.

Miss nothing;
Be like little children,
Able to see and enjoy those little seemingly insignificant
    things in life
Which really make up the whole of life:
        the wonders of nature,
        the beauty of a flower,
        the perfume of a rose,
        the song of a bird,
        the dew drops sparkling on the grass in the early
            morning,
        the glory of the sunrise,
        the gentle wind whispering in the grass,
        the raindrops trickling down a windowpane.

How simple
And yet how truly beautiful these things are
When you look at them with eyes that really see
And cease to rush through life
In such a hurry that you fail to notice them!

When you walk through the garden,
Do you see My wonders and beauties all around you,
Or is your mind so full of the cares and worries of the day
That you are blind and deaf and bowed down,
That you see nothing
For you are so wrapped up in yourself and self-concern?

Why not try today
To keep ever aware of all that is going on all around you?
Open your eyes,
Keep your feelers out
And really enjoy life.

When you can do this,
It means you are aware of the things that really matter,
That you are aware of Me,
For *I AM* in all those little things in life as well as the big ones.
You are aware of My divine presence in everything
And life can never be dull or mundane
When you are consciously aware of Me in everything around
     you.

Cease straining after anything
And simply allow things to unfold;
Do not allow worry to bind you and blind you
But learn to cast all your burdens upon Me
So that you are free to do My will and walk in My ways.

I cannot use you when you are tied up with yourselves
And cannot see the wood for the trees,
So let go,
Relax,
And do it now.

Be still
And dwell on the wonders of life,
Let your minds be stayed on Me.
Open your eyes,
See Me in everything
And give eternal thanks.

When you can see Me in everything,
Your heart is so full you cannot fail to give thanks;
It simply bubbles up in you
And flows over and out.
You cannot hide a heart full of love and gratitude
For it is reflected in your life and living for all to see.
When you are in a state of joy and thanksgiving
You attract others to you;
Everyone enjoys being with a soul who overflows with love,
For love attracts love.

Where there is love there is trust,
There is respect,
There is peace and harmony.
This can be in an individual,
A family,
A community,
A nation,
And so out into the world.
But it has to start somewhere.
It has to start in you.

Love is what makes the world go round,
It is what draws souls together,
It welds into one.
It is so strong that it is indestructible.

He who knows not the meaning of love is a misery to himself
And to everyone he contacts.
When there is love within the heart
It shines through the whole being.
The eyes are the windows of the soul,
Therefore love is reflected in the eyes and in the face.
The plainest person becomes beautiful when love is in that
        person's heart.

You cannot hide love,
It shines forth like a beacon of light enveloping all who
        are around—
Love of Me,
Love of your fellowman,
Love of your true self.

Love grows and blossoms like a glorious flower.
The more you love, the more you are loved.
The more love you pour forth the more love will be returned.

Do you know what it means really to love,

To feel your heart filled with such joy and gratitude that
        you cannot contain it
And it has to bubble over and out to all those around you?
It is a glorious feeling of well-being,
Of being at-one with all life.
All fear,
All hatred,
Jealousy,
Envy and greed disappear when love is there,
All irritation and annoyance melt away.
There is no place for those negative, destructive forces
In the presence of love.
When your heart is cold and you feel no love,
Do not despair
But look around
And you will find something you can love.
It may be some very small thing,
But that small spark can ignite your whole being
Until love is aflame in you.
Only a small key can unlock a heavy door;
Love is the key to every closed door.
Learn to use it
Until all doors have been opened.

Start doing this right where you are.
You do not have to go out into the world,
You will find there is plenty of work to be done right here
On your own doorstep.
Open your eyes,
Open your hearts,
See a need
And answer it.

You take the first step,
Do not always wait for someone else to do it.
You can always do something,
So do it without delay.

If you wait for someone else to make the first move,
You may have to wait a very long time,
Whereas you can do something about it right now
Without another moment being wasted.

Action!
Get into action
Create peace and harmony
By pouring forth love.

Into New and Uncharted Waters

I saw a dark, deep turbulent river. Then I saw someone standing on the bank wanting to get across to the other side, and the only way this could be done was by jumping from one boulder to the next.

I saw the person start, and in the beginning the going was very easy. Then he reached the middle of the river where the water was darker and more turbulent than ever, and the distance between the rocks was wider. I saw fear descend on the person.

Then I heard the words: "Be strong and of good courage. Take that jump in absolute faith and confidence, for I am with you."

I saw him take that jump and land on the other rock safely, and the look of joy and relief on his face was tremendous.

Fear not the unknown,
But move swiftly and confidently into it,
Knowing that only the very best will come from it,
That all those secrets which have been hidden are there
Waiting to be revealed
And that now is the time for these revelations.

You must be prepared for the most wonderful
And yet unexpected things to come about,
For all old molds to be broken,
All old conventions,
All those old links with the past
Which have held you bound and fettered.
You must be completely free to move into the New,
Having no ties with the past to pull you back.

Before you is the most wonderful and glorious future.
You are living by the ways of the Spirit
And it is the Spirit that leads you into the realms of the
        unknown,
Into the glorious New.

Only those who are strong and of good courage
Can move with complete freedom,
Only those who have real faith and belief,
Whose security is in Me.

Be not a doubter nor a waverer.
Let nothing throw you off balance;
Your foundations are built on rock,
They are built on Me.

You know that *I AM* with you always,
That *I AM* within you.
You know that when you have eyes to see
You can indeed see Me in everything and in everyone,
That *I AM* the Allness of All.

A group meeting in the gardens at Findhorn.

In the Findhorn children's center.

Eileen helping to cook for the community.

Peter and Eileen.

Be consciously aware of all this.
Let your minds dwell on the wonder of it;
Absorb it,
Let it sink into you,
Become a part of you,
So that you live it and breathe it.

Breathe in the truth of it
Then breathe it out into the world
So that more and more may become aware of it.

When you have found a real treasure you long to share it
    with all,
For as you share it
And give thanks for it,
It grows greater
And the joy in you is unbounded.

Hold nothing to the self
But share My good and perfect gifts
And never fail to give constant thanks for everything.

Do not make life complicated for yourselves,
Simply know there is an answer to every seeming problem
And let Me help you to find the answer.
Allow no blockages to develop and grow up in your minds.
Why not try what I tell you
And see how wonderfully it all works?

Have absolute faith
As you take that step forward to see if it works,
And expect miracles to come about:
Expect doors to open up,
Expect changes,
The most wonderful changes to take place,
For have I not told you that anything can happen
When your faith and trust is in Me?

Believe

And again I say believe,
For faith and belief are the open sesame into the glorious New
Which is waiting there for each one of you.

THE POWER OF FAITH

Where is your faith?
Where are your trust and belief?
Even if your faith is as a grain of mustard seed,
It will grow and flourish
And become strong and unshakable.

Faith grows
As you learn to demonstrate it
And live by it;
It grows
As you put it to the test
And put it into practice in your everyday life and living.

Faith has to be lived
Or it does not grow strong.
It is useless talking about faith
Or reading about it;
You have to live and demonstrate it.
The power is there for you to use
And draw upon at any time,
But unless you draw on it, it cannot flow.

You may have an electric light switch right beside you,
But unless you put your hand on that switch
And turn on the light,
You remain in darkness.
The light is there all the time
But you have to do your part by switching it on
In order to enable the current to flow.

So it is with faith;

It is there
Waiting to be drawn upon at any time of the day or night.

The greater the faith,
The greater the demonstration,
Until you realize that anything is possible
When your faith and belief are strong enough.

Do you really believe that anything is possible with Me?
Then it will be so.
It is a waste of time trying to work out the mechanics of
    faith with your mind;
It cannot be understood with the mind,
For it is of the Spirit
And therefore has to be accepted by the Spirit
And lived by the Spirit.

The ways of the Spirit are as utter foolishness in the eyes of
    men,
But instead of ridiculing this,
Why not try it and see what happens?

Take that step in faith
And see whether it really does work or not.
You cannot tell unless you try it.
You cannot learn to swim unless you take your toes off the
    bottom.
You cannot experience the full wonder and glory of this way
    of life,
Without living it.

This is something each individual has to do for himself.
You cannot bask in someone else's faith
Or live on someone else's faith.
You have to build up your own faith,
Step by step,
Until it is unshakable.

Never be lazy about this.

Be consistent,
And if something does not work out as you hoped it would,
Do not be downcast
Or allow your faith to waver.
Simply know that it is working out perfectly for all concerned
And only the very best will come out of it in the end,
That I know what is best for each one
And not just for you.
I hold the overall picture in My hands
And My plan is perfect.

You are living and working by immutable laws.
Fulfill the law,
Love the law,
And behold the amazing outworking of the law.
Know the meaning of complete freedom,
Because you are doing My will.

LET GO THE OLD, ACCEPT THE NEW

Let the old die away, revealing the new.
When a potato or a grain of wheat is planted in the ground
The old dies and rots away
So that the new can spring forth in abundance and glory.
Out of darkness comes great light,
Out of weakness great strength,
Out of death, life—life more abundant.

So let go of the old.
No longer try to cling onto it,
No longer try to nourish it,
But let it be transmuted into something entirely new.

Be not afraid of the new,
But accept it with full and joyous hearts

And know that there is something truly wonderful waiting to
    be revealed
When you let go of all the old completely.
The old potato is no longer part of the new;
It is left there, rotting in the ground
When the new potatoes are dug up.

Consider the wonder and mystery of nature
And know that there is nothing haphazard or ruthless about it;
It follows a perfect rhythm.
You are all part of nature,
Part of My creation.
Therefore see that you follow the perfect rhythm of nature
And do not try to pull or work against it.
If you do,
It will only cause great pain and distress
Which is not necessary
And will only hold up progress.

As you allow yourselves to let go
And work in perfect rhythm and harmony with all that is
    going on;
As you let all the old die and drop away without any resistance,
The new will evolve without any pain or disharmony.

Always remember that it is resistance that causes pain,
So learn to relax in My Love
And allow things to unfold in that perfect rhythm and
    perfection.

How much easier it is for a small child to accept the new
And really enjoy it,
Because there are no set and rigid patterns to be broken down
And changed before this can take place.
Why not become as little children,
Simple and uncomplicated,
And allow the wonders and glories of the new to unfold in
    your lives and living

So that there is nothing in you to hold up the perfection of it?

I keep telling you that life is so easy,
So simple.
Why must you make it so complicated?
Why torture yourselves when it is unnecessary?
Why not enjoy to the full everything you are doing?
Why not learn to do everything with Love and to My honor
    and glory?
Why not learn to bring Me into everything you are doing?

As you do this,
You will want to do what you are doing with great love and
    joy.
Things will no longer appear as burdens or limitations
But will be a real joy and pleasure
Because you are doing them for Me and not for anyone else.

ALL ARE PART OF THE INFINITE PLAN

You are all part of My infinite plan,
You each have a part to play in the overall picture.
It may only be a very small part,
Nevertheless it is essential for the completion of the whole.
Never at any time feel that your part is so small that it is
    not necessary.
Who are you to judge?
I need each of you in your rightful place
Playing your specific part.

Some of you may not have yet found out what your part is.
It is therefore up to each one of you to seek
And go on seeking until you have found out what it is
And then to go ahead
And do something about it.
Put it to use,
See why it works.

See yourselves fitting into your rightful place,
Giving what you have to give to the whole
And so feel part and parcel of that wonderful wholeness,
No longer separate or divided,
One in thought, word, and deed.

No one can do this for you;
You have to do your own seeking and your own finding.
No one else can live your own life for you;
Only you alone can live it.

Cease looking to others for help
Look for it within
And you will find it.
Always go to the source for the answer
And do not be satisfied with anything secondhand
Or anything that is not of the very highest.

What is deep within you is reflected without.
When there is law,
Order,
Harmony,
Beauty,
Peace
And tranquility within,
It will be reflected in everything you do, say and think.
Whereas if there is chaos,
Confusion,
Disorder
And disharmony within,
It cannot be hidden
But will be reflected in your whole life and living.

When change comes
It has to start from within and work out;
Then it will be lasting
And nothing will be able to throw it off balance.
You can start right now working on your own inner state.

You do not have to wait for anyone else to change,
You can do your own changing without any further delay.
Give constant thanks that you are able to do something
        about it without any hold-ups.
If there are any hold-ups
They are within yourself,
Therefore you are the one who can do something about them.

Do not sit back
And expect things to change in your life
But get into action
And do something about it.
Start from the bottom and work upward;
Then you will be cleansed and purified throughout
And can start off with solid rocklike foundations
Which nothing and no one can shake or destroy.

Once your foundations are sound
You can go on building and building without any concern.
See that your foundations are rooted and grounded in Me,
In the things of the Spirit,
On that which is from everlasting to everlasting
And not on the things of the world which are here today
        and gone tomorrow.
Live and move and have your whole being in Me.
Recognize this
And give thanks that it is so.

WASTE NO TIME REGRETTING THE PAST

Why waste time in futile regretting?
Why dwell on all your faults and failures,
On the things you have not done in life?
What does it matter if you have failed in the past?
What does it matter if you have made a real mess of your life?
What does matter is what you are going to do about it now.

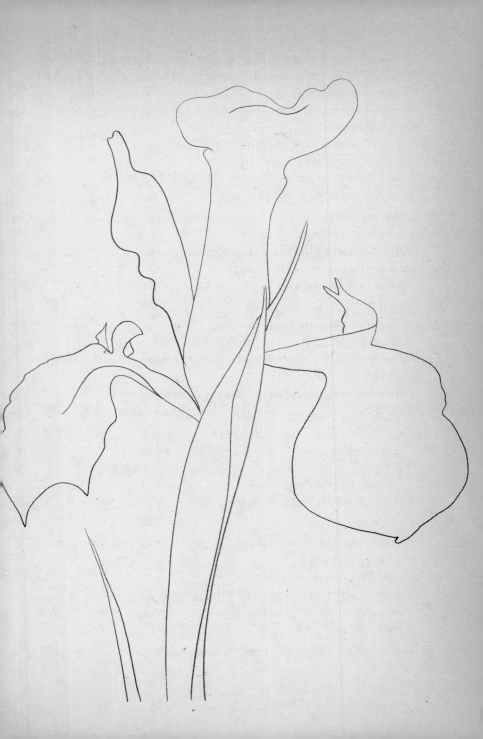

Yesterday you may have failed to put first things first,
You may have wandered off the straight and narrow path,
Going your own way.
You may have caused great distress and annoyance to your
        fellowmen,
To those who are nearest and dearest to you,
To those you work closely with,
But this does not mean that you are a complete failure
And that there is no hope for you.

Why not use those failures and mistakes as steppingstones
        to success?
Why not start right now righting those wrongs
And putting your house in order
And giving eternal thanks?

Today is a new day, a glorious day,
A day when you are going to succeed and are not going to fail.
Why not start off by giving thanks for today?
Why not look for and see the best unfold throughout the day?
Expect it to,
Do not even contemplate failure for one moment.

Start looking for the best Now.
Give thanks that you do not have to put this off until
        tomorrow,
That you can start right now living that glorious life which is
        your true heritage.
Enjoy this day to the full, leaving all regrets behind forever.

Can you do this?
Are you capable of forgetting the past instead of wallowing in
        it, in self-pity?
When you can do this
You are really learning to live in the moment.
In the ever-present, glorious Now.
This is the way I want you to live.

It is so difficult to work in and through you

When you are weighted down by self-concern,
Regrets,
Worries,
And anxieties.
You know this because I have had to remind you of it over
and over again.
Why not do something about it,
Instead of resenting the times I have to repeat these things
to you?

I can assure you
There is a very good reason for repeating them over and over
again.
Repetition is absolutely essential,
For only in this way do these vitally important lessons sink
into you.
And become a part of you
Until you find yourselves living them in your everyday living.

So be not impatient and resentful.
In order to teach a small child something,
You have to repeat it over and over again.
You may have to show that child how to do it many times
And see it fumbling awkwardly as it keeps on trying,
But you do not do it for the child or it would never learn.
You give it great love and encouragement
And are willing to stand back
And wait very patiently
Until eventually the child has attained mastery.
You must learn to master life.

THERE MUST BE CHANGE

Are you ready and prepared to change your ideas
And change your thinking?
Are you prepared to accept something new without
reservations?

Some can be really flexible
And do this with the greatest of ease,
But others have great difficulty
And this causes strain and stress in their lives,
Or it causes stagnation which is almost as bad.

Let none of you become rigid
And refuse to change and expand your consciousness.
You cannot hope to grow spiritually if you do,
You cannot hope to open the door to allow the new to enter,
Revealing wonder upon wonder to you.

Never be wholly satisfied with your outlook on life.
There is always something new and exciting to learn about
And you can only hope to do this if you keep really open
And very sensitive to all that is taking place.

The very new is not always easy to understand.
Do not allow this to concern you
But be willing to accept it in faith
And know that your understanding will grow as you do so.
You will know
By that deep inner knowing
Whether these new ideas,
New ways
And new thoughts are of the truth or not.
If you get that deep feeling of rightness,
Allow yourselves to absorb these truths
Even if you do not understand them fully.

Gradually the light will dawn,
And you will awaken to the meaning of it all.

You cannot go on for the rest of your lives in the same
    old way.
You must be willing to branch out into something new.
Never allow yourselves to feel
"What was good enough for my parents is good enough for
    me."

This is not progress
And there must be progress.

There must be change as you move forward into the
New Age
And this is what is taking place at this time.
Those who are satisfied with the old
And refuse to change
And accept the new
Will be left behind
And will indeed stagnate.

You must be courageous
And move forward into new ways
New and even uncharted waters
Without any fear.
I am guiding and directing you into those new and
unchartered waters
And I will not let any harm befall you.

Accept Me as your constant guide and companion.
Come to Me at all times
And let Me reveal to you the way, the truth, and the life.
You have not been asked to move in those uncharted waters
without your pilot.
I AM your pilot
And I will never let you down.
Trust me completely.

If the way is rough be not afraid;
If it is dangerous be not concerned.
I will guide you through it all.
But remember to let go and let Me do it,
And resist not.

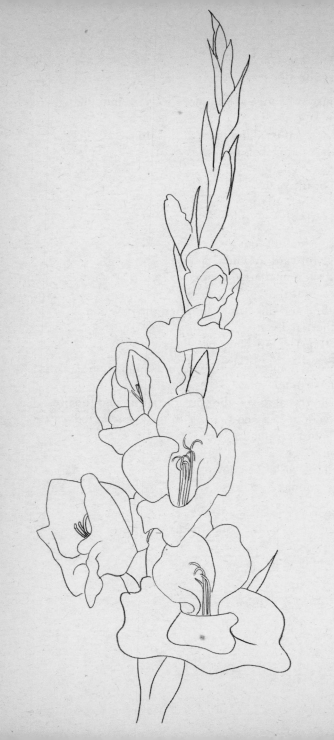

Through Thick
and Thin,
Through Rough
and Smooth

*A very high waterfall appeared. Many
floating objects were being swept over the
top of it and were plunging down into the
very depths where they seemed to
disappear. Then I saw that in time they
floated to the surface again and were swept
on their way.*

*I heard the words: "Never despair when
you are plunged down into the very depths,
but remember I am with you and when
you have been cleansed and purified I will
lift you up into My glorious Light and set
your feet on the right path."*

I will keep him in perfect peace,
Whose mind is stayed on Me.

Simply know that all is very, very well
No matter how things may appear outwardly.
You must have implicit faith that everything is in My hands
And that all is working out perfectly.

I want you to hold on to this through thick and thin,
Through rough and smooth.
It is your faith that will manifest on the outer plane
The perfection that is on the inner planes:
Faith in My perfect plan,
Faith that *I AM* with you always,
Faith that everything is in My hands.

Can you do this?
Can you hold the perfect before you no matter what is
    happening?

As you learn to do this
You will behold the most wonderful transformations taking
    place,
Because you draw to yourselves that which you hold in your
    consciousness.
When you hold success,
Abundance
And perfection in your consciousness,
You draw these things to you giving them form and substance.
Likewise if you hold thoughts of failure,
Defeat
And lack,
So will you draw those to you.

What are you holding in your consciousness?
Take time to take stock of yourselves.

What are you drawing to you?
The choice lies in your own hands, not in anyone else's.
I want only the very best, the very highest, for you.
If you choose of your own free will anything less
And draw it towards you
And are satisfied with second best,
There is nothing I can do about it.

Never be afraid to expect the best,
Never feel you are unworthy
Or are not justified in having the best.
I tell you this is your true heritage
But you have to claim it,
You have to accept it and expect it.
It is not demanding too much.

It is yours,
My gift to each and every one of you.
It is being held out to you.

What are you going to do about it?
Are you going to accept it with full and grateful hearts
Or reject it?
Let not false humility prevent you from accepting what is
    yours by right.

And do not just accept it,
But glory in it,
Give eternal thanks for it.
Treasure it
And watch the wonder of it unfold in your lives,
Knowing without a shadow of doubt that all that I have is
    yours.

Remember always to put first things first in your lives,
And never try to grab anything to the self.
If you do
It will bring you no joy

And will wither away into nothingness.
Get your values right.

This is one of the fundamental lessons you all have to learn
And the sooner it is learnt the better.
Until you have learnt it
You cannot expect everything to go right for you;
And even that which you have will be taken from you
Until you put Me first.

ALL THINGS ARE POSSIBLE WITH GOD

Let the power of the Spirit flow in and through you.
Open yourselves to this infinite power
And realize its true secret lies in keeping in close
      contact with Me,
In drawing from that infinite, eternal source.
It is always there to be drawn upon
By all who are ready and prepared to use it aright
For the benefit of the whole.
You have to be ready;
You have to ask before you can receive.
It will not be pushed upon you before you are ready.

"Ask anything in My name,
Believing,
And it is yours."
You have to believe,
For it is your faith and belief which draws it to you.

Never forget at anytime
That you carry your success or failure with you
And that it does not depend on outer conditions.
You are your own master;
Therefore never blame your failures on anyone else,
But search your hearts

And find out what it is within you that has caused the failures,
Then right them as quickly as possible
And move on to success.

Do you believe that with Me all things are possible?
Do you accept this as fact
Or do you still allow doubts and fears to spoil the perfection
    of your lives?
What is your attitude,
Your outlook?

Take time to ponder on this
And see where you are falling short.
See your shortcomings clearly so that you can rectify them
But never at anytime become disheartened by them
Or they will master you instead of you mastering them.
I would have you master of your true destiny,
Triumphant and victorious,
On top of every situation no matter how seemingly impossible.

By your right and positive attitude
You can very quickly overcome all difficulties and all obstacles.
Do not just sit there
And expect them to solve themselves for you
Without you doing your part by right thinking and right
    attitude.

"Seek and ye shall find."
Seek the solution,
Seek an answer and it will be yours.
This does not mean that you go ahead and take action
    unguidedly,
But it does mean that you wait upon Me
And when you receive the green light to go ahead
You do so without any hesitation,
Without any doubts and fears
And watch everything working out perfectly.
The timing must be perfect,

Then everything falls into place.

There is perfect rhythm in all life
And when you are in rhythm you flow with it without any
    effort,
And will find such joy and upliftment in so doing.
So why not get into rhythm,
Get into tune
And enjoy life to the full?
Cease struggling and exhausting yourselves.

OUR REFUGE AND OUR STRENGTH

I AM your refuge and strength,
A very present help in times of distress and trouble.
Learn to call upon Me,
To lean upon Me,
To draw from Me,
To put your whole faith and trust in Me;
And as you do so
See every difficulty and problem dissolve into nothingness.

There is the perfect answer to every problem,
Look for it and you will find it.
Waste no time wallowing in your problems and self-pity,
But rise above them
And give thanks that the answer is right there
When you expand your consciousness
And have faith that the answer is there
Waiting to be put into action
When you can still your mind.

"Be ye transformed by the renewing of your mind."
You can turn a grim situation into a really wonderful one
By changing your whole attitude towards it.
You can change your attitude towards a person

By changing your thoughts towards that person,
By replacing negative, destructive thoughts with loving,
    positive constructive ones.

You can solve every problem
By simply knowing that the answer is there
When you can become still
And take time to seek and find it
And cease running round in circles getting nowhere.

It is in the stillness that all will be clarified;
It is in the stillness that you become at peace
And can find Me.
I am always there;
But you are blind to this wonderful fact
Until you can become still
And seek Me in the silence,
And this you can do at all times.
The more often you put it into practice
The more natural it becomes
Until you can do it as naturally as breathing.

You do not have to rush off to be by yourselves to find me.
You will be able to find Me at all times
And in everything you are doing.
It does not matter what chaos and confusion are all around you
Nor what outer noise there may be.
You can go into that inner peace and silence
And find Me.

When you have found Me
The Light of truth will shine on every situation,
For where *I AM* there is no darkness,
There are no problems.

What a lot of time and energy are wasted
Because you do not take the time or trouble to be still!
It is the secret solution to every situation.

Surely you know this by now,
For you have been told it often enough?

Why not prove it to yourselves
By putting it into practice to see how it works?
When you learn to live this life I keep telling you about,
You will see how wonderfully it works.
Until you try something
And put it to the test
It remains a theory.
This life is a very real and practical one,
A life of action.
There is nothing theoretical about it,
But it is up to you to do something about it to prove that
 this is so.

The daylight is there,
But until you pull back the curtains you remain in darkness.
Water is in the tap
But until you turn on the tap and let the water flow
It remains static.
Food can be sitting there on your plate,
But until you put it into your mouth and eat it
It does you no good.
Get into action; do it Now.

NEVER WASTE TIME IN SELF-BLAME

Why condemn yourselves for your inadequacies,
Mistakes,
Faults,
And failings?
Why not,
Instead of dwelling on the negative things in your lives,
Turn those weaknesses into strength
And faults and failings into virtues

By looking for the positive
And allowing the positive to express itself in your lives
    instead of the negative?

This is something each individual has to do.
Deep within each one of you,
You will find real beauty, virtue and goodness.
It may be hidden very deep in some
And may need a great deal of uncovering to draw it forth,
But have faith that it is there
And you will find it when you search for it with real
    determination.

When you refuse to see the best in yourselves
And choose to dwell on all the negative things within you,
You must be willing to accept the consequences,
For you draw to yourself what you hold in your thoughts.
Think the very best
And you will draw the very best to yourself.
Know that you can do anything
When *I AM* with you, leading and directing you,
And you will be able to do it.

As you think, so you are.
You have heard those words so many times;
Now let them become living words
And see them become fact in your lives and living.
See your thoughts live and move and have their being in you
And know that My words are not empty.

You expect the very best,
Therefore you will see the very best.
When you accept that *I AM* within you, how could it be
    otherwise?
There must be an acceptance of these wonderful truths,
An awareness of them.

Never waste time feeling you have a very long way to go in
    this spiritual life.

Instead be encouraged and strengthened by realizing how far
	you have come,
And give eternal thanks for that.

Realize how much you have to be grateful for.
Surround yourselves with beautiful thoughts,
With beautiful things,
With beautiful people.
See the light shining in everything and everyone.
Let your light shine brightly from deep within you
And know that nothing without can extinguish it,
That only your own negativity can do that.
Therefore keep positive all the time.
More and more light is needed in the world,
So keep your lights burning brightly,
Each and everyone of you,
So they can blaze forth pushing back the darkness.

Always choose the path of light and ignore the darkness,
Thereby giving it no strength.
Light and darkness cannot abide together
So make your choice.
When you have nothing to hide
It will be your greatest joy to dwell in the light the whole
	time,
So it can shine in and through you
Bringing light and more light into the world.

Lift up your banners on high, My light bearers!
More and more souls are joining the ranks of light bearers
As the hunger for spiritual food grows greater in the world.
The glorious light will meet the need;
It will show the way
And more and more souls will find true freedom and joy
As they enter the light and move forward in it.
Be light
And let it shine forth from you.

Be love and let love flow from you freely
And help meet the tremendous need in the world.

THE BEST IN LIFE CAN BE YOURS

It is up to each individual
To set the higher powers,
The spiritual laws,
Into motion.

It is a waste of time thinking about them
Or talking about them:
You have to do something about them to attract the very best
        to you.
It is no use sitting there with your hands folded in your lap
Hoping everything will drop into them.
You must set into operation those higher forces and powers
By taking hold of them,
Doing what has to be done
And doing it well,
Knowing that you can do it,
That there is no such word as "can't."

Why not affirm,
Believe,
Expect,
Know,
That you can do all things with Me
And go ahead in confidence and faith and do it?

See the world at your feet,
See the very best in life as yours
To use for the good and benefit of the whole.
Never be satisfied with second best.
Always remember that all you are doing is for Me
And to My honor and glory,

Therefore only the very best will do.
Your only desire is for the very best for your Beloved.

As you learn to live in this way,
        putting Me first in everything,
        loving Me with your whole heart,
        feeling the closeness and Oneness of our union,
You will never be satisfied with just anything.
Your aim will always be for the very best
And when the choice is placed before you,
You will know what your decision should be,
So make the right decision without hesitation.

You are in the world but are not of it.
There is no need to allow the things of the world to drag
        you down.
Enjoy them,
But do not try to possess them or allow them to possess you.

In the New Age it is not necessary to wear sackcloth and
        ashes;
It is not necessary to go around declaring that you are a
        miserable sinner
And are not worthy to be called My beloved child.
All this is of the old age
And is false
And unreal.

Accept that we are One,
That *I AM* within each one of you.
Feel yourselves being lifted out of the darkness of all this
        false teaching
Into the glorious Light.
Leave behind all the old,
Let it die a natural death
And enter the New reborn in spirit and in truth
And know the meaning of true freedom.

I need you free,
Not all tied up with self and self-concern.
Be like a very small child,
Free and joyous
With no concern for what tomorrow may bring
And live in the ever-present now.
You can live a far more effective life in that way.

Why waste time trying to work out the rhyme and reason
     for everything?
My ways are not man's ways,
Therefore it is a complete waste of time and energy
Trying to work them out with the mind.
Simply be willing to accept them
And give eternal thanks for them,
Enjoying life to the full.

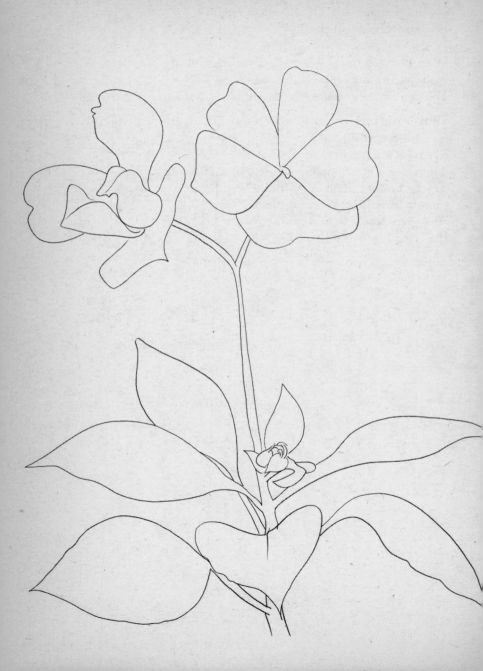

Listen and Hear My Voice

I was aware of a great noise all around and then the noise died down and there was great stillness. In the stillness I could hear what seemed to be the faint ticking of a clock. As I listened very intently, the sound became louder and clearer.

Then I heard the words: "I am always here but unless you become consciously aware of Me and of My divine Presence, you cannot hear My voice. Therefore still that which is without so that you can hear that which is within."

Listen,
Listen,
Listen,
And then you cannot fail to hear that still small voice
    within you,
Which is My voice
And the most wondrous and most precious gift
Which I hold out to all mankind, but so very few accept
    it as fact.

It took you a long time to accept it in this way,
But now it has become a part of you.
You know you can turn to Me at any time of the day
    or night,
And you can hear My voice,
But you have to make that conscious effort to do so.

A good example of learning to do something consciously
And only being aware when you do so
Is listening to the many wonderful sounds all around
    you all the time;
For example the birds always singing their hymns of praise
But you only become aware of the real beauty of their song
when you stop
And listen.

You are surrounded by so much beauty
And yet you fail to see it
    until you stop
    and consciously open your eyes
    and see that beauty
And yet it is there all the time.
You could see it unceasingly if you chose to do so,
But instead you go around with the blinds pulled down.
Let in the Light

And see things as they really are in their full glory
     and beauty.

So with My voice;
It is always there,
Therefore listen,
Become very sensitive towards it,
So you do not miss My slightest whisper,
For I do not shout from the housetops.

I am within each one
And I speak from within.
Is it any wonder you have to be ever conscious of Me
     and of My voice
And concentrate fully upon it so you miss nothing?

When you have heard what I have to say to you,
The next step is to obey
And carry out My instructions without hesitation.
Why listen to advice
Or ask for advice
If you do not do something about it?

This is what happens so often.
You ask My advice about something
And I tell you what to do,
And somehow it does not seem to fit into your scheme
     of things;
It may sound a rather strange piece of advice
And you hesitate and ponder over it,
And the more you allow your lower mind to dwell on it,
The more ridiculous it sounds,
Until in the end you push My advice aside
And decide to take things into your own hands
And do it your way.
Then when you do that and things do not work out as you had
     expected,
You become annoyed and upset.

When you have sought My advice and I have given it to you,
Go right ahead
And act upon it immediately.
Then you will really see My wonders brought about in the
    most amazing way.

Obedience is vitally important,
Therefore listen
And obey at all times,
And bring down My kingdom on earth.
When you find yourself wandering away from Me down some
    byway,
Pull yourself up,
And come back onto the highway,
And follow that way.

I am there to guide every step,
Therefore listen
And "follow thou Me."

TRUE PRAYER

What does it mean to you to "pray without ceasing,"
To be consciously aware of Me and of My divine presence?

Why not take time and ponder on this.
Life without prayer is empty and meaningless
For it is that quiet, silent prayer,
That communion with the higher part of you,
Which reveals to you the fullness of this glorious life
Which is your true heritage.

Let your prayers be very positive and constructive,
And always give thanks for what you are about to receive
Even before you pray for it.
As you pray,
Feel a Oneness,

A unity in all life where there is no separation,
For all is One.
Prayer unites all;
It draws all together
And creates that perfect Oneness.

Talk to Me
And listen to Me.
Never waste time in beseeching Me for this, that, and the
    other
For that is not true prayer.
To beseech is to create separateness
And I want you to create Oneness at all times.

We are One,
I AM within you.
You do not have to search for Me without,
I AM always there
Waiting for you to recognize Me
And to cease your eternal quest for Me.
Recognize our Oneness now,
I in you
And you in Me.

You can call upon Me at any time
And you will always find Me there,
Ready to help you in every way.

Learn to bring Me into every department of your life
So that you share everything with Me,
Your faults and failings
As well as your victories and triumphs.

I AM your Beloved
And when you truly love
You long to share all with the Beloved.
Never try to hide anything from Me;
It is the truth that sets you free
And I need you free.

The more open you are the freer you are.

It is when you are trying to hide something
When you are ashamed of your failures,
Of your fears and doubts
That you are not free
And become tied up with the little self
And so separate yourselves from Me.

Banish all fears
And doubts
And replace them with Love,
For where there is Love there is no fear:
       love Me,
       love your fellowman,
       love what you do,
       love where you are,
       love those that hate you and despitefully use you,
       love your enemies.

Let My divine Love radiate in and through you
Until there is no room in you for anything negative or
      destructive
And Love reigns supreme in your lives.

Start doing this now.
Start in the small things in your lives,
And see this wondrous Love grow
And grow
Until you see nothing but the very best in everyone and
      everything
And you *KNOW I AM* in all things and in everyone,
That all is One.

LIVE IN HARMONY WITH LIFE

Get into tune with what is going on.

To begin with you may not even be fully aware of what it
      is all about.
It is something you feel within,
Vibrate with,
Feel in harmony with.
You have a feeling of expectancy
Of excitement.
It is in the very ethers,
The air you breathe,
The ground you walk on.

You have felt a similar feeling when Spring has been in the
      air,
A bursting forth of new life.
It is all there just waiting to come forth,
And before you realize what is happening
Spring is there
And you are in the middle of it.

The New is here
And you are in the middle of it,
You are part of it
And find yourselves vibrating with new life
All the old has passed away.

It is a glorious feeling of complete freedom and abandonment,
Of bursting out of the old confined ways into new
      spaciousness
Where there are no limitations.
You can feel yourselves growing and expanding in every
      direction
With a feeling that anything can happen at any moment
And you are ready for it,
Ready to move right into it.

You are like a runner at the starting line,
On your toes
All keyed up,

Ready to be off at the starter's signal.

There is so much going on
At all levels at this time
That you cannot help being aware of it.
Changes are coming
And you are part of those changes
So go along with them.
Be willing to change
And change quickly when and where necessary.
Do not hesitate or hang back;
Step right into all that is taking place
Swiftly
And surely
And with absolute confidence and faith.

Realize there is perfect harmony and rhythm in all that is
    taking place,
Nothing is out of tune
Or out of timing.
It is a glorious unfoldment
Nothing can go wrong
And all is very, very well.

Spring unfolds in true perfection:
This is the Spring of the New Age
And this too is unfolding in that same true perfection.
Simply go along with it all
And help to speed up the process,
Giving constant thanks
That you are part of it,
That you are aware of it
That you are at the spearhead of all that is happening.

There is no turning back now.
You must go forward,
Ever forward,
Towards the glorious goal.

Light bearers unite
And let your lights blaze forth!
The greater the unity,
The greater the Light.
More and more Light is needed in the world
And you are all part of that glorious Light,
So hide not your Light.
Every single Light is needed to increase the power and
    strength of it
So that nothing will be able to withstand it.
Light will envelop all
And darkness will be no more.

RAISE YOUR CONSCIOUSNESS

Only as you expand your consciousness
Are you open and receptive to the new all around you
And can become attuned to new thoughts,
New ideas,
New ways of life.

Be prepared to see beyond the immediate into higher
    dimensions,
Higher realms,
And open to the ways of the spirit.
There is so much you can understand and accept intuitively
But at which the mind boggles
So why waste time trying to work everything out with the
    mind?
Why not be willing to live and act intuitively and
    inspirationally?

When you do this
You are functioning from a raised state of consciousness
And are receptive to the new.

You become a clear channel for the new to unfold in and
through you.

Raise your consciousness,
  from the negative to the positive,
  from the destructive to the constructive,
  from the darkness into the light,
  from the old into the new
And see what happens.

You will find the old will fall away revealing the glorious
new.
You will find yourselves seeing the world around you with
new eyes,
You will behold the wonders and beauties,
As the scales of the old which have held you in bondage will
fall from your eyes
And you will see with eyes that really see.
You will look with wonder and thanksgiving at all you see
And realize that this is indeed the new heaven and new earth
About which you have heard so much;
That it is right there before you
And you are part of it;
That you live and move and have your being in it
And are helping to bring it down
And bring it about.

You will see that you as an individual have an important part
to play
In bringing the new to birth,
  that what you do,
  how you behave,
  how you live,
  how you think
All fits into either a constructive or a destructive pattern.

When each individual realizes this fully
And sees that he has a responsibility to the whole,

This transformation from the old to the new will come about
more quickly.

Never try to shelve your responsibilities
Or leave them to someone else,
But accept them joyously
And see your part in the whole scheme of things
And be willing to play your part without any thought of the
self.

Let all you do,
Say,
And think
Be for the good of the whole,
To lift and build up the very best in every situation.

Be willing to learn
And learn quickly how to do this,
So that you are a blessing to your fellowman and to the whole
situation.

Give eternal joy and freedom as you do so.
"Walk in the Light"
And radiate it wherever you go,
Creating more and more Light.
Look for the very best and draw it to you.
These are constructive things you can do
And can do Now;
So waste no more time thinking about them
But put them into action.

BE OPEN TO THE TRUTH

Keep wide open,
Have no preconceived ideas regarding the way, the truth, and
the life,

Simply know that when you keep open and allow truth to
    enter
It is the truth that sets you free.
But unless you open yourselves to the truth
It cannot enter in
And reveal the way to you.

You hold the key,
You have to unlock the door,
But once you have done that,
Truth can do the rest
And reveal to you the way to life,
Life eternal,
And a whole new world will open up for you.

Let not intellectual pride,
Nor preconceived ideas,
Opinions,
And prejudices
Lock and bar the way,
Nor close yourselves to truth
Because it does not come through conventional or orthodox
    channels.
It is so easy to slam the door on truth
Because it is revealed through some unusual and unorthodox
    means.

You are moving into the new
And therefore you must be prepared for many new ways and
    means.
When a child is moved into a higher grade in school
It has to learn many new lessons,
New methods;
In fact it has to learn to expand,
To be able to take in and accept all the new subjects it has to
    learn.
So it is with moving in the New Age.

You cannot hold on doggedly to the old
And refuse to expand your consciousness to accept something
    entirely new
Simply because you are afraid that if you do so
It might disrupt your nice conventional, smooth-flowing life
And turn everything upside down.
You have to be willing to branch out,
To try new experiments,
To step out into the unknown.
You have even to be willing to make mistakes
And learn by those mistakes,
Knowing that as you do so you will keep growing in wisdom,
And knowledge,
And understanding,
Preparing yourselves for even newer and more wonderful
    revelations
To be revealed to you.

Do not be concerned;
You will not be moved up from the first grade straight into the
    sixth grade.
Step by step the way will be revealed to you.
You will gradually be moved into higher vibrations
So that they do not overwhelm you;
And as you become attuned to them,
They will be stepped up a little more.

This is what is happening to so many of you at this time.
You know something is happening to you,
But you are not always sure what it is all about.
You find yourselves becoming more sensitive to what is going
    on all around.
You are aware of the things of the spirit,
Of the things that really matter in life.
You find yourselves
        feeling things very deeply,

> opening up your hearts,
> loving as you have never loved before,
> doing things you never felt you were capable of doing.

Let go;
Do not be afraid and try to put the brakes on.
This is all part of the process of moving into the New.
Therefore give thanks that these things are happening to you
Because it means that you really are moving,
Changing,
Being stepped up,
That you are not any longer stuck in a rut.
Growing and expanding is an uncomfortable process at times,
But a very necessary one,
Let it not disturb you
Or get you down,
But unfold with it into the glorious new.

DOING GOD'S WILL

As you learn to do My will and walk in My ways
You will begin to know the meaning of peace and harmony
> within.
Your hearts will overflow with love for one another,
Your understanding will expand,
You will become more tolerant and open
And see clearly that there are many ways and many paths
> which lead to Me,
The Center,
The Source of all life.

You will learn to live and let live
And no longer feel that your way is the only way.
You will never again be dogmatic about anything,
But very quietly and confidently go your way
Doing what you feel is right for you

And will never try to interfere with anyone else's life.
You will no longer try to change other souls,
But will learn to live in such a way
That others will want to know what it is you have got that
    they have not.

It is by your fruits you shall be known,
Which is why it is so vitally important simply to live a life.
You can help more souls by just being and living
Than by talking,
                talking,
                    talking.
So much time is wasted by discussing,
Analyzing,
Criticizing,
And when this takes place actual living is forgotten.
Never forget you can teach far more by example.
How you live
And how you quietly go about doing My will,
Will have far more effect on mankind
Than shouting many wonderful words from the rooftops
And failing to live what you preach.

It is useless to say you love someone
If you fail to express that love in the way you behave towards
    him.
Love should be expressed
But it should also be lived and demonstrated in many small
    ways,
So that the beloved feels that love
And is secure in it.

The more love you pour forth
The more is returned to you.
You can never really love someone
Without love being returned to you sooner or later.

When you do not see immediate results,

Never close your hearts
But keep the love flowing all the time
And know that sooner or later it will bring its own reward
      in its own special way,
And it will be tremendous when it comes about.

Be faithful and constant in pouring forth love and more love.
Just go ahead and do your part
And leave the rest to Me.
It is I who work wonders in and through all those who are
      ready and responsive.

Love opens up hearts,
Even the hardest of hearts,
So never despair of anyone.

Learn to act from deep inner promptings
And do not waste time going around asking advice from the
      many
Which will only cause chaos and confusion within you.
When you really want to know the answer to something
You will find it,
But you must learn to be still
And wait upon Me
And then when you know what to do,
Do not hesitate to do it
But have the faith to know that it is right
And therefore everything will work out perfectly
Not just for you,
But also for all those concerned.

LET YOUR LIFE BE GUIDED BY ME

When you know that you are doing the right thing
And are in the right place
And that your life is being guided by Me,

Peace and serenity enfold you
And all strain and conflict roll away from you like the
      outgoing tide
You can go ahead
And do all that has to be done
With a wonderful sense of peace and rightness.

You will find this taking place as you learn to wait upon Me
And cease rushing ahead and acting impulsively.
Wait,
Wait,
Wait
Rather than do something without My blessing,
But once you are aware of My blessing
Go ahead in complete confidence
Do what has to be done,
Knowing that only the very best will come out of it,
Not only for you but also for all concerned.

Many times you may have to go ahead in faith
Unable to see the full reason for the action you are taking,
But do not hesitate when you know within that it is right;
You thus allow the most wonderful pattern to unfold.

You must have faith to be able to take steps into the unknown,
For there may be many outer influences pulling you this way
      and that
Until you feel torn to pieces.
This is where you have to learn to go within;
And know with absolute knowing that what you are doing is
      being guided by Me
And is right,
Therefore look neither to the right nor to the left
But go straight ahead
And do what you know has to be done,
Knowing it will work out perfectly.

Once you have taken a step in the right direction

Never turn back,
For if you do it will be like turning your back on the light,
And walking straight back into the darkness.
He who has put his hand to the plough must not look back
But go forward fearlessly,
Full of expectancy,
Knowing that all is well.

It takes a great faith and courage to step out
And follow those deep inner promptings,
Especially when the action you are taking appears as utter
    foolishness in the eyes of man.
That is why you could not do it without complete faith and
    inner knowing.

The choice always lies in your hands:
Therefore choose
And choose aright
With your hand firmly in Mine,
And waver not along the way.
I will never fail you nor forsake you
But will guide your every step,
So be at peace.

As you go forward one step at a time,
You will become more and more aware of Me and of My
    divine presence
And you will realize that of your own strength you could not
    do what you are doing.
You will be able to see My hand in all that is taking place
And your hearts will be filled with deep love and gratitude.
You will grow strong in My strength and wisdom
And accomplish the seemingly impossible.

Give thanks,
Give constant thanks,
For everything.

"Abide in Me and I will abide in you."
Keep consciously aware of Me and of My divine presence,
Then nothing can separate us.
We are united in that Oneness,
And peace and harmony reign in your hearts.

Let nothing distract or distress you.
Find that peace which passeth understanding
And remain in it.
Do My will
And walk in My ways.
Take time to find out what My will is for you.
Go into the silence
And wait upon Me
And know that as you do this
I will reveal to you the way, the truth, and the life,
Then it is up to you to do something about it
And walk in it.

Another soul can only take you so far along the spiritual path.
The rest of the way you have to go alone,
And the sooner you realize this
The quicker will you be able to move forward.
Never try to cling to anyone else
And hope that you will be able to reach the goal in their glory.
You have to do your own spiritual work.
You have to do your own searching in your own way.
You may all have different methods of doing this,
But this does not matter.
The result will be the same in the end.

Be not critical of anyone else's way or method.
Just be concerned about your own
And how you are going to reach the goal.

When you are doing this you will not have time to be critical
"Judge not that ye be not judged."

You may know all this in theory,
But it is not much good unless it is put into practice.
That is why I have to remind you over and over again to live
      your own life.
There are many of you who resent this constant repetition.
The answer to that is to get on
And *do* something about it
So that I do not have to keep on repeating Myself.

I will have to go on and on
Until all you are learning becomes a part of you
And it lives and moves and has its being in you.
So be not despondent,
Just get into action.

This is a life of action,
A life of change.
Let there be no complacency,
For when you are complacent
You can so easily get into a rut which creates stagnation.
See where you need to change.
And then take the action necessary to bring about that change.

If change is uncomfortable,
The more quickly it takes place the easier it is.
It is far less painful
To pull a bandage off quickly than to do it slowly.
Therefore do what you know has to be done
Without wasting any time thinking about it
And wondering about it.

Take that leap into the New without hesitation
And simply know it will be wonderful,
Far,
Far more wonderful

Than what you have left behind in the old.
With change comes life,
A full and glorious life.
It is being held out to you.
Take it
And give eternal thanks for it.

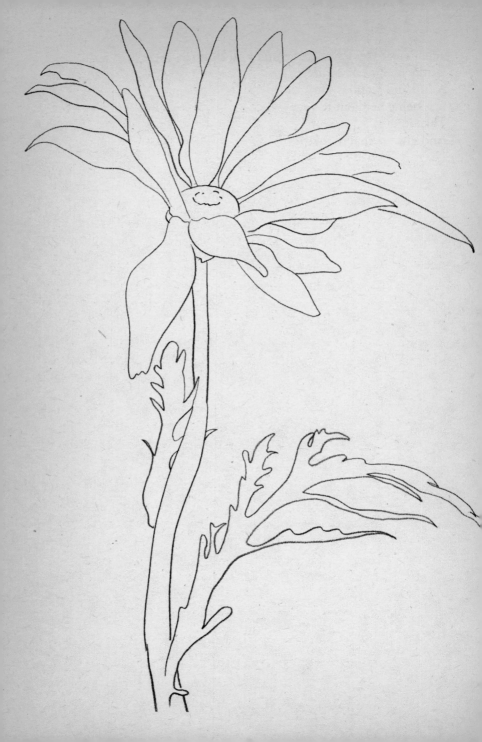

The New Heaven and the New Earth

I was shown great light descending from the heavens and great light ascending from the earth. I watched the two come together, blend, and become one.

I heard the words: "Behold, this is My new heaven and new earth. It is here now, but it is up to each one of you to help to give it form and substance."

Awake refreshed and renewed,
Ready for anything, expecting the very best from the glorious
      day
And therefore receiving only the very best.

Relax and let Me take over.
Never start the day strained and full of tension.
Sleep and rest renews the spirit and revitalizes it.
Start the day off on the right foot
Without any stress or strain
But with a heart full of love and gratitude,
Full of great expectations for the new day.

Today has no blemishes on it to mar it,
So why not keep it like that?
Keep your consciousness raised to the highest
And see the most wonderful things unfold this day.

This is a new day and a new way;
Leave yesterday behind with all its faults and failings
And turn over a new page.
Why drag the old behind you into this new day?
By all means learn your lessons,
But why dwell so much on those lessons that they become too
      heavy
And drag you down
So that you cannot enter the new with a light and joyous
      heart?
Why become so heavy with remorse and self-concern
That you can hardly drag one foot in front of the other.

Did you wake up this morning with a heavy feeling
Wondering how you were ever going to get through the day,
Dreading it?
This is no way to approach the day
And if you did happen to have started off in this way,

Why not change your whole attitude
Right now
Without another moment's delay.

Give thanks that you can change in the twinkling of an eye,
That what looked really dark and gloomy a few seconds ago
Can change completely as your attitude changes.

Look for that silver lining and you will find it.
Look for the answer to that problem that was weighing you
    down
And you will find it there staring you in the face,
In fact you will wonder how you could have been so blind
    not to have seen it before.
It is so clear and obvious.

How vitally important your right and positive attitude is
    towards today
And all that it holds for you!
You can make or mar the day for yourselves
Simply by the way you approach it.
If you feel the world is against you
And that nothing will go right for you,
This is just what you will get
And you have no one to blame but yourselves when this
    happens.

Your reactions to things as they take place can make all the
    difference.
When your reactions are negative and aggressive
You immediately put up barriers
And create opposition
And find yourselves finding fault
And blaming everyone else for the mess everything is in.
You are so blind
You fail to see that you are the one at fault
And you go around with a chip on your shoulder.

When your reactions are positive and constructive
All barriers come tumbling down
And you will find you will get help and cooperation from
    every side.
If you have made a mistake admit it,
Say you are sorry and move on.
Then no precious time is wasted in trying to justify yourselves
And prove you are right.

You all have many lessons to learn
Learn them quickly
And try never to make the same mistake twice.

ALWAYS GIVE THANKS

As you listen to the bird song in the early morning,
You find a great sense of peace and joy.
The very first thing the birds do
When they waken at the crack of dawn
Is to open their little hearts
And sing their song of joy and thanksgiving.
Their first thought is one of thanksgiving.

As you learn to live closer to nature day by day,
Your relationship with Me,
The Lord your God,
Will become more and more real
And more and more joyous.
The birds do not have to be taught to love Me
And to recognize Me their Creator;
They are simply aware of Me,
They know it
And sing their song of praise to Me.

Let yourself sink into the simple things of life,
Absorb the beauties all around.

When you become very sensitive and aware,
Even a blade of grass becomes a truly wonderful thing as you
    observe.
But you have to open your eyes
And open your heart to be able to absorb all My wonders
    which are all around you.

"He that hath eyes, let him see,
And he that hath ears, let him hear."
Every man has eyes and ears,
Yet all men see what is before them in a completely different
    way.

When you take something for granted,
Whether it is a person or a thing,
You find all the sparkle goes out of life
And out of that person or thing;
It becomes dead.

When you cease taking things for granted,
You begin to look at them with new eyes,
You see what appeared to be dull and uninteresting has come
    to life;
        it is sparkling,
        scintillating,
        a wonderful jewel:

    you stare at it in wonder
    you touch it in true reverence,
    you lift up your heart
    and thank Me for it
For you know and realize that all good and perfect gifts come
    from Me.

You become childlike in your wonderment.
That is the way life should be all the time,
Full of wonder and glory,
And so it can be when you learn to see things as they really are

And take nothing for granted.

No one likes to be taken for granted over anything.
I never take My children for granted;
Walk in My footsteps.
Live as you know I live,
Treat others as you know I treat them.
Then life becomes new, becomes wonderful.
You see a purpose and plan running through everything,
Nothing can become dull and uninteresting because your eyes
     are open,
Your ears are open,
You are alert,
Eager,
Looking for beauty
And therefore seeing it at every turn.

There is beauty all around for those who choose to see.
Choose aright all the time,
Let there be less and less lapses into the old, dull dreary life.
Advance steadily into the new,
With your head uplifted in deep deep gratitude and
     thanksgiving.

When your eyes and ears are open to My wonders,
You are truly living in the new.
You are alive in Me.

LOVE ONE ANOTHER

Can you truthfully say you love your fellowman,
That you are really interested in him,
That you appreciate him
And know him as your brother?
Or do you just tolerate him
And find it a real effort to have to rub shoulders with him?

You cannot say you love Me if you do not love your
	fellowman,
For relationships are so closely interwoven
That it is impossible to love one without the other.

Do you spend time picking and choosing whom you are going
	to love
And whom you feel you could not possibly love?
There should be no discrimination in love,
For divine Love embraces all alike,
Sees all men as brothers,
All as My image and likeness,
No matter what color, race, creed or religion.
You will have to reach the point
When you can really see and understand the Oneness of all
	life,
Know the true meaning of the brotherhood of all men
And know Me as the Father of all.

Many can accept My Fatherhood
But find it very difficult
And even impossible
To accept their brotherhood with all.
This separation is the cause of all the trouble and chaos in
	the world.
The cause of all strife and wars.
Only when man can accept all as his brother
With Me as his Father
Can there be lasting peace and tranquility in the world.

The place to start putting things right is in yourselves
And your own personal relationships
With all those with whom you come into contact.
Cease pointing your finger
And being critical of those with whom you cannot get along in
	the world,
Those with whom you cannot see eye to eye.

Put your own house in order.

You have more than enough to cope with yourselves
Without tearing your fellowman to pieces,
Pointing out all his faults and failings
And where he has gone wrong.
When you are willing to face yourselves
And put things right within,
You will then be able to help your fellowman simply by your
    example,
Not by criticism, intolerance, and many words.

Many times I have told you that actions speak louder than
    words.
What are you doing about it?
Are you learning to live a life
And put this into practice
Or are you still talking about it
But failing to do anything about it?

I tell you there is far too much talk and discussion in the
    world
And not nearly enough action,
Not nearly enough positive constructive living.

Love your fellowman as I love you,
Help him,
Bless him,
Encourage him,
See the very best in him.
"Do unto others as you would have them do unto you."

PERFECTION IN ALL THINGS

Do not dissipate your energies.
There is so much to be done,

But you must learn to channel your energies in the right
    direction
And not fritter them away by dabbling in many things
And many activities.
It is so easy to do so
And this is where self-discipline is necessary.

You have to seek and to find what you should be doing,
Where you are going
And then go straight ahead
And not be tempted to try your hand at a hundred and one
    different things and ways.
You need variety
And you need to be very flexible,
But this does not mean a dissipation of energy.
It is far better to learn to do one thing
And do it perfectly
Than to indulge in many things
And do them badly.

This is where some of you will have to watch yourselves
    carefully.
There are those among you who are like butterflies
And like to flit from one thing to the next,
Imagining that variety is the spice of life,
But you do nothing well
And perfection is not your aim.

Learn to do what you know you can do perfectly.
Let your standards be of the very highest
And if you do not feel you are giving of your very best in what
    you are doing,
Be willing to change in midstream
And find out what your capabilities are.

I ask you not to be a dabbler in many things
But a perfectionist in everything you undertake.
If necessary be willing to be instructed

Until you have really mastered what you are doing.
Be willing to learn
And never feel that you know all the answers,
There is always something new to learn.

Find out what you have to give,
And give it wholeheartedly.
Never forget that there are many, many levels on which to
     give.
Therefore each individual has to find out in which way
And on what level
He can give of his best,
And then give it.

Never try to be like someone else.
You may have a unique gift
And you will be unable to discover what that gift is
If you are modeling yourself on another person.

Seek within
And you will find what you have to give.
There are many parts to a body
And every part is necessary for the smooth running of the
     whole.
In a community there is need for many different types
To make up the perfect whole.

That is why I have drawn together such a variety of different
     individuals,
Each with something specific to give to the whole.
If you still feel like a fish out of water
And are not quite sure where you fit in
Or what you have to give,
Then take time to be still
And seek
Until you have found out what it is.

Only you can find that out,

Do not expect someone else to tell you,
This is an inner knowing.
I tell you all who are drawn here have something special to
    contribute.

THE JOY OF TRUE GIVING

As you give so shall it be given unto you.
The more you give the more you will receive.
Your very giving draws forth giving
So give
And go on giving
Expecting nothing,
And yet you will find it will be returned to you in good
    measure,
"Pressed down,
Shaken together
And running over."

The joy and delight of giving is tremendous.
As you learn to give
And give wholeheartedly
Of the gifts and talents which are yours—
You each have different ones
And they all function on different levels—
So will you grow in grace and stature.

If you have a happy, sunny nature
And you give of that wherever you go
It will be returned to you a thousandfold,
For everyone responds to a sunny disposition.

Always remember "as you sow so shall you reap."
If you sow criticism,
Intolerance,
Disloyalty,

And negativity,
You will reap these for you draw them to you.
Why not start right now sowing seeds of joy,
Happiness,
Love,
Positiveness,
Goodness,
Tenderness,
And understanding,
And see what it will do to you.
Your whole outlook on life will change
And you will find that you will draw the very best in life to
    you
And the joy you reflect will be reflected by all those around
    you
For everyone loves a joyous giver
And responds to that giving.

Never at any time feel that you have nothing to give.
You each have a tremendous amount to give
And you will find that the less you think about it
And the more you just live it,
The better it will work.

The more you are thinking and living for others
And can forget the self completely in service to others,
With never a thought of what you can get out of life,
The happier you will be.

Never at any time give with one hand and take away with the
    other.
When you give something,
Whatever it may be,
Give it with no strings attached
So that it can be used completely freely.
This applies to all giving.
It is so limiting when a gift is given with conditions attached.

And you will find it will take all the joy out of it,
For the giver as well as the receiver.

When you give
Let your giving be done abundantly,
Freely,
Wholeheartedly
And then forget about it.
Do not hark back to your giving
For if you do that is not true giving.
Never give something
And then later on want it back
But let it go completely,
It is no longer yours,
This applies to gifts on all levels,
Whether material or spiritual,
Tangible or intangible.

Always be generous in your giving
And never be afraid of suffering lack,
For again if you do,
This is not true giving.
With true giving you will lack nothing.

THE LAW OF ABUNDANCE

Simply accept
With a heart full of love and gratitude
That all your needs are being wonderfully met,
That I know exactly what they are even before you voice
      them.

Why not start right now thinking abundance
And realize that there is no virtue in being poor?
You can do so much more
When you can accept that all I have is yours

To use for the good of the whole
And do not limit yourselves in any way.
When you can accept the true freedom of the spirit,
You can shake off all sense of limitations,
All sense of lack,
And learn to use all you have with real wisdom,
Understanding that all I bestow upon you must be used to
    My honor and glory
And that you must be good stewards of all My good and
    perfect gifts.

I remind you every now and again to think big,
To expand your consciousnesses
And to see all My wondrous promises coming about.

It is necessary for you to do your part in the overall plan
By being ultrapositive about everything,
By seeing the very best at all times.

I want you to understand that money as such is neither good
    or bad;
It just is;
It is there to be used
And it has to be kept circulating and not hoarded.
It is power,
And power has to be handled wisely.
You do not handle electricity foolishly,
For if you did it would destroy you,
So why handle money in an irresponsible manner?
Never love money for money's sake
But know that it is the love of money that is the root of all
    evil,
Not money itself.

It is necessary for each one of you to start thinking in terms
    of thousands,
Not hundreds,

Not for yourselves but for the whole.
Until you do
You cannot expect to draw thousands upon thousands to you,
And you need this to help you to expand in every direction.

It is necessary for this My Center of Light to grow and expand
And this is happening at great speed.
Feel yourselves grow and expand with it,
Feel the real joy and excitement as this takes place.
Feel part of the whole
And so give of your very best to the whole.

When your heart is in everything you do
And you really love all that is taking place,
You will only want the very best.

Know that there is an answer to every problem,
And every problem will be overcome
Far more quickly than you ever dreamed of.
Have faith,
Know that I go before to prepare the way
And that I make the crooked places straight and the rough
     places smooth
And that with Me all things are possible—
All things.

Behold My wonders and miracles
And give eternal thanks
And take nothing for granted.
Enjoy everything to the full.
It is a wonderful,
Wonderful life
And you are all mightily blessed and greatly privileged to be
     alive at this time,
Doing what you are doing,
Ushering in the glorious New Age.

Unity in a group is vitally important.
You each have to learn to work together perfectly
Like the fingers on a hand.
You each have your different roles,
And they are entirely different
So you need never try to copy anyone else.

You are all individuals
Very specially chosen and trained by Me
To do a specific work which only you can do,
You can each help each other when help is needed,
But the actual work has to be done by you.

This unity does not just happen;
You have to bring it about.
The thing that unites you is your relationship with Me
First and foremost.
When you are all doing My will,
You will find you are drawn together by invisible threads,
Therefore keep stretching towards Me all the time
And know that when you feel a sense of disunity with your
          group,
It is because your relationship with Me is not right
And hasten to do something about this.

I want you to watch out for this,
And when you notice even the slightest rift,
Do not waste time wondering why
Or wishing that someone else would do something about it,
Look within your own heart
And you will soon see where you can start to put right what is
          wrong.

Recognize that disunity stems from within your own heart.

This is something always to be remembered
And as your group grows,
You have to become ever more watchful.
When you have a large group of individuals gathered
    together
Working together,
Unless they realize what it is that binds them and keeps them
    together
There will always be trouble.

The secret is to find and retain that complete Oneness with
    Me,
Know that we are One
And that *I AM* within the very center of your being.
Keep that relationship right
And all else will fit into place perfectly.

In the old it was so much easier to live for yourself
With no consideration for anyone else.
You did not have to think of anyone else,
The lower self was in complete dominion,
But now life is entirely different.
Never again can you live for the self,
You live entirely for Me
And your whole living stems from our relationship
And only perfection can result.

So always take action when necessary,
You can always do something,
There need never be any feeling of frustration.
As you raise your thinking
And think on Me
And My work
And My will,
You help those around you to do the same.

There is a great need for really stable and dependable souls,
Ones who are always in the right place at the right time
Doing what needs to be done,
Living in such a way that nothing upsets them
Because they are in complete control of every situation,
And live and act from that inner center of peace and stillness.

Their security is in Me,
Therefore nothing can throw them off balance.
They know what they are doing
And why they are doing it
And have a real sense of responsibility.
They can be completely depended upon to see a job through
No matter what it is
And to see it through perfectly.

Search your hearts:
Are you really dependable,
Have you a sense of responsibility
So that you really see a job through to the end
And never leave anything half done?
Are you always in the right place at the right time,
Or is your timing way out?
Do you have to be reminded over and over again
Before you finish a job as it should be finished?

It is important that you really take time
To see where you are missing out
And then see what you can do to rectify it.
Never be satisfied to let things slide,
For if you do,
You will find things will gather speed
And before you realize what is happening
They will be out of control
And you will be completely overwhelmed by the situation.

Never allow things to get on top of you
But keep well on top of them.
Be master of every situation.

In the New Age really responsible, dedicated souls are
        needed,
So learn your lessons quickly.
Why learn them the hard way when you can do it the easy
        way?
How you learn them is up to each one of you:
I can show you the way,
But you have to follow it.
I can point out the alternatives
But you have to make your own decisions.
No one is going to push you one way or the other;
You are all free agents.

When you long to do the right thing
And take the right path,
You will do so.
You must be strong
To be able to withstand the temptations which may beset your
        way,
And to recognize them for what they are.
Every temptation overcome gives you a deeper inner strength
        and stability,
Making you able to face anything without wavering.

My ways are very strange
But remember that I see the whole of the picture
Whereas you only see such a small portion of it.
I see all the actors in the play of life,
You see only the ones nearest at hand.
There are many you have not yet met.
One by one I point the way to them
And they follow it
And take their part in the whole vast overall plan;

And so the plan unfolds in true perfection.

Watch it unfold
And glory in the wonder of it.
It is so wonderful that it is past understanding.
Just be willing to accept it all with full and grateful hearts
And see My hand in everything.
Never at any time fail to see My hand in all that is taking
place.

TRUE PEACE IS WITHIN

Release all strain and tension
And let Me express My infinite abundance in and through
you.
I know your every need even before you ask
And your every need is already being wonderfully met
Your needs on all levels from the greatest to the smallest.

You have to expand now
For the ball has started to roll
And nothing can stop it.
This Center of Light can no longer remain hidden away;
The whole world shall know about it.
The news of it
And what is taking place here
Is spreading like wildfire
And people will flock from all over the world to see what is
happening.

Souls are hungry and desperate
And are seeking an answer to all the chaos and confusion in
the world at this time.
Day by day it grows worse
But be not afraid
For things will have to get worse before they can get better.

A boil comes to a head before it bursts
And all the poisons are released and are cleared away.
Things have to come to a head in the world
Before the poisons of hate,
Greed,
Jealousy,
Selfishness,
And all those negative poisons are released
And cleared away
And healing can take place.

Simply hold on
No matter what outer appearances may be
And know that all is very, very well,
That things are working out.
It is not easy to do this,
But this is where your faith and trust have to be strong
And you must believe what I tell you
And know that My every promise is coming about.
The timing must be right.

There is a tremendous cleansing taking place.
It is essential,
Do not resist it
Or fight against it,
But seek that inner peace and stillness deep within which
      nothing can disturb
And remain in it.

This can be likened to the eye of the hurricane
Where there is perfect peace in the midst of chaos and
      devastation.
Nothing will be able to touch those who can find that inner
      peace and stillness.
"A thousand shall fall at thy side
And ten thousand at thy right hand,
But it shall not come nigh thee."

Believe these words with all your heart and soul
And see the wonder and truth of them,
For this is exactly what happens to those who truly love Me
And put Me first in everything
And find that secret place deep within
From where peace and harmony will grow without.

It is important you do not become involved in the chaos in the
      world
But seek and find that inner sanctuary,
So that you can be a help and the answer,
Instead of becoming part of the disease
Which is everywhere rampant at this time.

I need you at perfect peace within.
You will find this as you keep your minds stayed on Me
And can raise your consciousness
And look far,
Seeing the very best
And concentrating on that.

I have to keep on stressing this,
Because it is so vitally important.
You cannot help the world situation
If you allow yourselves to become involved in it.
You have to be immune to the disease
Or you too will contract it
And then you can be of no help whatsoever.

I need your help
I need you free,
I need you at perfect peace:
Then I can use you.

Hold the vision of perfection,
Harmony
And beauty
Ever before you
And see it in everything and everyone.

Let the Love within bubble over like water
And flow to all alike.
Let there be no discrimination in you,
For all are of Me,
All are one family.
Accept that brotherhood of man,
And the fatherhood of Me, the Beloved.

Universal Love starts within each individual
And works its way out.
When each individual realizes this
And allows that Love to flow freely,
Great changes will come about in the world,
For it is Love that transmutes all hatred,
Jealousy,
Envy,
Criticism,
Greed.
These are the qualities that cause war, destruction and death.

Love creates life,
Life everlasting,
Life abundant,
And brings with it peace,
Joy,
And true and lasting happiness and contentment,
And above all unity and oneness.

Accept your Oneness with all life,
Accept your Oneness with Me.

Do not shy away from it
Feeling you are not worthy to accept this Oneness.
This feeling of unworthiness is what separates man from Me,
    His Creator.
For too long mankind has been told he is a miserable sinner
And is not worthy to walk and talk with Me.
For too long he has separated himself from Me
Until he no longer knows Me,
No longer realizes that *I AM* within him,
Nearer than breathing,
Closer than hands and feet,
That *I AM* there
Waiting to work in and through him when he will let Me.

Banish forever all these false teachings and false concepts of
    Me.
I AM Love.
I AM within each one of you.
        "I AM THAT I AM."
Accept with joy and wonderment our Oneness
And be ye perfect even as *I AM* perfect.
Accept it as a very small child
And do not waste time and energy trying to analyze it
And work it out with your minds.

If you try to approach this wonderful life intellectually
You waste much time
And will want to try out many devious routes
So that you will fail to see the simplicity of it
And the direct approach which is there for all who are willing
    to accept it.
My ways are simple,
Cease making them complicated for yourselves.

If you have wandered off into the highways and byways
And have lost your way,
Come back,

Come back to the straight and narrow path
Which leads straight to Me
And there you will find Me
Waiting deep within you.

Those who have eyes to see,
Let them see the wonder and simplicity of this life I am
      holding out to them
And let them accept it with real joy and thanksgiving.

Have I not told you that My Kingdom is come,
      My will is being done—
        that the new heaven and new earth is here Now,
        that all my good and perfect gifts are yours,
        that we are One?

Simply open your hearts and minds
And accept all
And become one with all that is coming about
And expand
And expand
All is very, very well.